Imperfekt

ALSO BY TAB EDWARDS

Paper Problems

"Coffee *is for* Closers ONLY!"

I&O: Imaging & Output Strategy

MPS: Managed Print Services

Lessons *of the* Navel Orange

Batman, Robin, David Beckham,
and the Naked King

Chocolate Peppers

The Art *of* Movement

TAB EDWARDS

Imperfekt

TMBE

TMBE, PHILADELPHIA, PENNSYLVANIA 19129

TMBE / *Media*

ISBN 978-0-9909866-0-7

This publication is designed to provide authoritative information in regards to the subject matter covered. It is sold with the understanding that the publisher is not engaged in rendering legal, accounting, or other professional services. If legal advice or other expert assistance is required, the services of a competent professional person should be sought.

   —From a declaration of principles jointly adopted by a committee of the American Bar Association and a committee of publishers.

Tab Edwards books are available at special quantity discounts to use as premiums and promotions, or for use in corporate training programs. For more information, please visit the website TabEdwards.com.

Designed by Water Creative
Philadelphia, PA.

1   3   5   7   9   10   8   6   4   2

TTX

CONTENTS

I exist
Therefore, I am
I am = I'm = Im
Imperfect = Perfe<u>k</u>t
("Perfect," imperfectly)
I am Perfekt = I'm Imperfect
I'm Imperfect = ImPerfekt
ImPerfekt = I exist imperfectly:
An acknowledgment; an opportunity

THE $2 DINNER BELL

"Jeezus! That was excruciating!"

"That's an understatement. After a while, it was tough to watch."

"I counted 112, what did you get?"

"I got 134!"

"By the 15-minute mark, I wanted to throw the poor woman a life-line."

"Out of sympathy, someone should have thrown her *the hook*."

"Well, that'll probably go down as the shortest-lived promotion in history."

"Yeah, you're probably right."

"It's too bad. I really think she's talented."

"I agree, but not when she's speaking in front of an audience."

These were comments from the crowd that exited the meeting after listening to newly-promoted marketing executive "Jill" address a crowd of more than 100 of her peers, subordinates, managers, and company executives. They were commenting on Jill's presentation at the company's quarterly meeting. It was Jill's first presentation since being promoted only a week prior. Whip-smart and an effective marketer, Jill had harbored a secret that she had been able to hide until asked (told) to deliver that fateful presentation: she was horrified at the thought of standing in front of an audience and giving a presentation. Jill suffered from an anxiety known as *glossophobia* (a fear of public speaking), a condition which, according to the National Institute of Mental Health, 74% of people share. One-on-one, she's fine. But, the idea of standing in front of a crowd, especially an audience of your new subordinates, peers, and managers, gave Jill nightmares. During the presentation—which I witnessed—Jill exhibited all of the classic symptoms of stage fright: increased perspiration, shaking hands, dry mouth, difficulty speaking, and—most damaging of all—an apparent lack of confidence, which affected her credibility and her perceived leadership qualities by the people whom now reported to her.

Jill was so nervous that, among other glossophobia signs, she repeatedly used the interjection, "umm." So much so, that the people sitting next to me started counting the number of times she said "umm"; someone counted 140 of them in the relatively brief presentation.

The day after the disastrous presentation, I received a phone call from one of the executives at Jill's company.

"Hey, Tab. This is David Miller."

"Hey, David. What's up?"

"I want to ask you a favor."

"Shoot. What do you need?"

"You are by far the best presenter I have seen in many years, so I am coming to you first. Would you be willing to work with Jill to help her become a better presenter? As you saw, she didn't do so well yesterday, and her new managers are already forming unfavorable opinions of her. She's a talented marketer and a good person, and I don't want to see her management career derailed simply because she's not a good presenter. As an executive, she will have to deliver lots of presentations, so she needs help, and fast. This would be a favor to *me*. Can you help?"

"Say no more, David. I'm in."

A few minutes later, I received a call from Jill. We talked for a few minutes and agreed to meet to discuss the presentation skills improvement work that she and I would be undertaking.

The next week, Jill and I met. When embarking on any type of improvement initiative, whether it is a business process improvement initiative, a sales improvement initiative, or—in this case—a presentation and public speaking improvement initiative, I always begin the process by defining what we are trying to accomplish through the initiative. By defining goals and objectives, we can then develop specific action plans to give us the best chance of accomplishing these goals and fulfilling the purpose for the improvement initiative.

I asked Jill "What do you want to accomplish by this skills improvement initiative?" Jill answered that she wanted to become a "better presenter," to which I replied "What do you mean by a 'better presenter'? If you only uttered 100 'umms' during a presentation instead of the 140 'umms' from last week, would that mean you were a 'better presenter?' Is that what you want? Why do you want to become a better presenter?" Jill went on to explain that becoming a better presenter would lead to what she really wanted: to erase the memory of her admittedly-terrible presentation from the minds of her subordinates, peers, and managers, thus helping her to re-establish credibility as a leader. This became the goal toward which we worked. The way to achieve this was to make sure that Jill "killed it" at the next manager's meeting at which she had been asked to present; the meeting was two months away.

I started the first skills improvement session by asking Jill to deliver (to me) a 10-minute slide presentation about her high school. As Jill delivered the presentation, I took notes on everything that detracted from her presentation's effectiveness: she fidgeted with her hands; her mouth was dry; she lost her place in the speech; she shifted uncontrollably on her feet; she had poor eye contact; she started noticeably sweating; her PowerPoint slides were a mess; and, she said "umm" a lot. In total, I counted twenty-five problems with the presentation and her delivery. At that point, we were ready to start working on correcting problems.

Our next skills session was held two weeks later. For that meeting, I brought a few helpful tools with me: a $2 dinner bell, a printout of the Boys & Girls Clubs of America's clasped-hands logo, breath-mint strips, masking tape, and a Batman & Robin comic book. First, I gave Jill the breath-mint strips: "Eat one of these before you present. It will eliminate your dry mouth." Next, I gave her the Boys & Girls Clubs logo: "This is how I want you to hold your hands while you present." Then, I gave her the comic book: "You are Batman and your PowerPoint slides are Robin. Batman is the focus; Robin supports Batman. Your presentation slides should never be the focus of your presentation. They should always be 'Robin'." After that, I used the tape to mark a few "X"s on the floor to show her where to keep her feet to eliminate the foot-shifting problem. And finally, the dinner bell. Each time Jill uttered an "umm," I rang the bell to make her cognizant that she was saying it too much. By becoming aware that she was saying "umm" a lot, she was able to dramatically reduce its use. Initially, however, I hit the bell so many times that people thought there was a fire drill in the building.

Jill's presentation skills improved dramatically with each session, to the point that she was actually looking forward to delivering her redemption presentation in two weeks.

Then, it was go-time. Jill allowed me to preview her presentation before she delivered it and she was fantastic. During the dry-run presentation, I noted only two issues with the presentation and her delivery: (1) she forgot to put a period at the end of one sentence, and (2) no one at the upcoming meeting would believe it was the same Jill. I was really proud of how far she had come, how hard she had worked, and how much she had improved as a presenter.

After the presentation, I received two text messages:

"Killed it!!! THANK YOU!" (from Jill)

"She killed it!!! THANK YOU!! (from David)

Soon, word got around that I had "performed a miracle" by turning Jill into a fine presenter, and I began to receive lots of requests from people—some business-related and some personal. In addition to the usual "We'd like you to help us streamline our operations process" and "Can you help me improve my sales performance?" types of requests, I received several requests asking for help with personal, non-business related goals. One person asked if I could help him manage his workload so that he could spend more time with his family, and another person asked if I could help him improve his reputation within the company. One person even asked me if I could help her develop a plan to improve her grades (she was taking evening and online courses to complete a college degree); and believe it or not, I did. I worked with her to develop a plan to improve her grades while balancing work and home life, and she ended the semester with two As and one

B grade; this was an improvement from the prior semester when she had earned two Cs and one "Incomplete."

After having worked with various people on both business and personal improvement initiatives, I noticed something interesting: the same principles that applied to helping businesses and organizations perform better also applied to helping individuals:

1. Acknowledgment that "something" in the current state is unsatisfactory and/or does not meet one's expectations or aspirations;

2. Identification of the unsatisfactory "something;"

3. A genuine desire to accomplish something significant related to that which was identified as unsatisfactory;

4. A plan to accomplish that significant "something" and an execution of the plan;

5. Adjustments to the plan based on progress toward or success at accomplishing that significant "something."

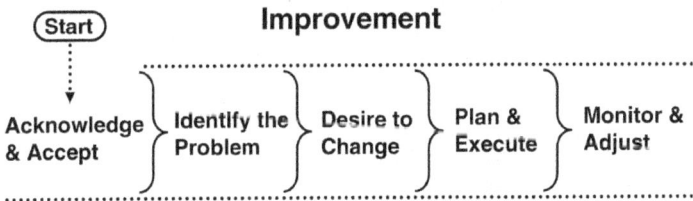

Improvement

Start → Acknowledge & Accept — Identify the Problem — Desire to Change — Plan & Execute — Monitor & Adjust

After having applied this "Model for Improvement" in various situations to help people achieve personal goals over the years, I have amassed significant evidence—*proof*—that these concepts are successful at leading individuals to become better at whatever their pursuit. "Can you help me position myself for a promotion at work?" Yes, I can. "Can you help me become more appealing so that I can find a partner?" Sure. "Can you help me start up a small business?" Absolutely. "Can you help me achieve perfection?" Hmm. Perfection. That one puzzled me. Or more accurately, it *stumped* me.

How would I go about developing an Improvement Plan to help someone achieve perfection? "To improve my presentation skills" is one thing, but to "achieve perfection" is quite another. The basic approach for developing an Improvement Plan is as follows:

1. Define the *goal* to be achieved (for example, "To fit into the blue jeans that I wore in college");

2. Define measurable *objective(s)* that will determine whether the goal has been achieved (for example, "To lose 10 pounds within 3 months"; the logic being that if you lost 10 pounds you would fit into your college blue jeans);

3. Develop an *action plan* to accomplish the weight-loss objective (for example, "Eat only vegetables; drink lots of water; have dessert only once per week; jog 1 mile each day; take the stairs").

Developing an Improvement Plan for organizations and individuals utilizing this approach is rather straight-forward, as long as the desired goal is realistic and attainable. Is achieving perfection realistic? Is it attainable? How would I know whether or not the person with whom I was working had actually attained or achieved perfection? It's easy to know whether a person is successful at fitting into their college blue jeans: you put them on and pull the zipper. If the zipper zips easily, congratulations; if not, cut back on dessert. But, perfection is not a pair of pants, it's … I can't even describe *what* it is. Most likely, the person hoping to lose enough weight to fit into the pair of college blue jeans is really looking to improve his or her health, physical "attractiveness," or sense of accomplishment. But, what is the perfection-seeker actually looking to become or to achieve?

For the first time in my life, I really spent time thinking about perfection in a person, a person's condition, or a person's endeavors. What would a perfect person act like, look like, think like, believe, know; what would a perfect person BE? To help me through this thought process and to formulate a foundation of perfection, I tried to think of other things that are "perfect"; just because I could neither think of what a perfect person would be nor any examples of people who were perfect, I thought, surely, there must be *something* that is perfect from which I could glean the characteristics of perfection. A perfect man; a perfect woman; a perfect book; a perfect meal; a perfect house; a perfect car; a perfect school; a perfect teacher; a perfect sweatshirt; a perfect pair of blue jeans—*something!*

If I was to somehow work with this person to help her achieve "perfection," I had to determine the parameters of

perfection so that we could define exactly what she ultimately hoped to accomplish and how she would know that
she had indeed accomplished that thing or those things that
would determine her perfection. Okay, I thought, here's an
easy example that might yield some clues: practically every
person receives schooling or attends school at some point
in our lives, and when we do, we all strive to get "perfect"
grades. So, I figured, by identifying what makes someone's
school grades perfect I would have some easily-obtainable
clues about how to begin to define perfection.

Most commonly, a student's final grade in a particular
class or course is based on the scores the student achieves
on examinations and assignments (for objectivity, we will
exclude subjective things like "class participation"). If, for
example, a tenth grade school teacher creates a math exam
with ten questions worth 10 points each, for a total possible
score of 100 points (or 100% correct), a student will complete a "perfect" exam if the students correctly answers all ten
questions, achieving a score of 100 points or 100%; perfect.
And if the student performs the same feat for each exam she
completes in each of her different classes, the student would
have achieved a perfect report card showing straight-As. In
this example, perfection would mean doing everything correctly, without mistakes.

But what does that mean, exactly? Does it mean that
the test-taking tenth grade student is perfect (flawless in
her understanding) of tenth grade math, English, history,
and science, or does it just mean that the student turned in

"perfect" scores on her exams earning her a "perfect" report card? How can achieving a perfect score on an exam that was created by an imperfect person (the teacher) mean that the student has achieved perfection when the imperfect teacher's opinion of perfection is flawed by virtue of the fact that the teacher is imperfect?

A major challenge with a student's perfect test score of 100 points being an indicator of that student's perfect understanding of the subject matter is *relativism*—specifically, the comparative nature of testing as an indicator of knowledge and understanding. If, for example, the hypothetical test-taking student in the aforementioned example attends Tomorrow's Builders Charter School in East St. Louis, Illinois (rated by AOL My Finance as the "worst performing public school in the U.S.") achieves a perfect score of 100 points on the math exam—indicating that the student has a "perfect" understanding of tenth grade math based on that teacher's and that school's expectations—does that mean the student would also have a perfect understanding of tenth grade math at Philadelphia's Saint Joseph's Prep (one of the country's most academically-rigorous institutions)? The answer is *no*. This means that test-score perfection is relative based on the school, the teacher, and other conditions, leading me to conclude that achieving perfect grades is not a universal indicator of perfection.

But what about college admissions and placement exams such as the time-tested American College Testing (ACT) exam which are more universal, rather than school-, demographic-, or state-specific? Surely, such an important, influential, scientific exam must be a perfect determinant of "college readiness" for students who achieve a perfect 36 (the top composite score), wouldn't it? Developed in 1959, the ACT college readiness assessment is a curriculum- and standards-based tool that assesses students' academic readiness for college. The exam consists of four multiple-choice tests: English, Mathematics, Reading, and Science (and an optional Writing Test). The ACT test is taken by more than 1.8 million high school students every year. Nationwide, just one-tenth of 1 percent of ACT test-takers achieve the top composite score of 36. In 2013, just 1,162 of 1.8 million students earned a 36.

To develop the test, the ACT incorporates the objectives for instruction for American middle and high schools, reviews approved textbooks for subjects taught in Grades 7–12, and surveys educators on which knowledge skills are relevant to post-secondary success. Each year, the ACT contracts with item writers to construct test items; the item writers are content specialists in disciplines measured by the ACT tests. Certainly, any student who achieves a perfect score of 36 on this heralded exam is a safe bet to have achieved perfect grades (straight-As) in school—or, maybe not. As just described, the ACT's questions are developed by imperfect people who—due to their imperfection—cannot create anything that is perfect. This idea is supported by an article in *The San Diego Union-Tribune* featuring five students who achieved perfect scores on the ACT exam. One of the students stated that, "Doing well is often largely a matter of test-taking skills rather than actual skills," [she] said. "Even a brilliant student can get a lower score than someone who's used to taking the tests." Well, so much for the veracity of the ACT exam as an indicator of perfection.

Trying to identifying the parameters of perfection in test scores or class grades provided me with no clarity about how to define perfection elsewhere. But surely, something must be perfect, shouldn't it? A perfect marriage? Nah. Turns out that the only people who believe someone has a perfect marriage are the people not actually in the marriage which they believe to be perfect. A perfect body? Nah. People can't agree on whether a man's perfect body type is closest to that of 3-time Mr. Olympia winner Phil Heath (5'9" tall and 275 pounds of hard muscle) or top male supermodel David Gandy (tall, slim, and lean); and we can't agree on whether a woman's perfect body is closest to that of actress Scarlett Johansson (realistic, "normal," and attainable) or that of a supermodel (6' tall and 125 pounds). A perfect woman's shoe? Nah. Try telling an 80-year-old woman on a budget that the $6,400 Christian Louboutin Daffodile 160 crystal-embellished suede pumps with the 6.5-inch heel are perfect. The perfect food? Nah. Although milk was once referred to as the "perfect food," according to *USA Today*, 60% of adults cannot digest milk (lactose intolerant). A perfect sports team? Nah. In the National Football League (NFL), the 1972 Miami Dolphins remain the only team in the modern era to have a "perfect" season—by NFL standards. They completed the season undefeated at 12 wins and 0 losses; they won each of their playoff games and eventually won the Super Bowl Championship, ending with an unblemished 19-0 record. But, upon retrospection, was their season *really* perfect? I say it was not. A perfect season would be a *flawless* one: no games lost; no incomplete passes by the quarterback; no penalties against them; no points scored against them; no yards gained against their defense; and no players injured, for example. If these parameters define perfection in a football team's season, then the 1972 Miami Dolphins did not achieve it.

Try as I might to identify something—anything—perfect, I found it to be a difficult and fruitless task. Test scores, grades, marriages, foods, shoes, nothing that I could think of helped me define any meaningful perfection parameters that I could use to develop a plan for helping the perfection-seeker in her quest to achieve it. My pursuit led me to believe that maybe there is no such thing as a perfect person, or a perfect meal, or a perfect painting, or a perfect anything. But that's ok, because, ultimately, when a person expresses a desire to be perfect or achieve perfection, they want perfection for a *reason*. And, as a consultant and a coach, it has always been my job to help the person define the reason(s) and develop a plan to achieve the goals for which the reason(s) is merely symptomatic.

When you get right down to it, people who seek perfection don't really want perfection per se; instead, they want what perfection would provide them. The man, who wants to lose 50 pounds and achieve a perfect body, doesn't ultimately want a perfect body at all; the man wants what having a perfect body would bring his way: better health, the respect of others, or to attract a companion, for instance. The student's ultimate goal is not to get a perfect score on the ACT exam, but is instead, *to get into the college of their choice*. And since there are lots of factors that college admissions boards use to determine admission, the scores on the ACT exam, the SAT exam, or even one's grades in high school are merely *objectives* which will help students accomplish their ultimate goal of getting into their first choice college. My job is often to help people and organizations understand that point: Is it perfection that they ultimately hope to achieve or accomplish, or is their desire for perfection a condition or prerequisite for something else they hope to achieve or become? Getting people's buy-in to this idea is often easier said than done. Many people I speak with do believe that perfection is an achievable goal or attainable state. So, for these people, the first step in our quest to develop a plan to help them is to have them articulate what, exactly, they are asking for when they say they want "perfection," and what they aspire to when they say they want to be "perfect."

1

CHAPTER ONE

Person, Place, *or* Thing

PERSON

Here's a challenge: Name a person whom you believe is "perfect." Who, in your opinion, is that "perfect person"? Who is that perfect teacher? Who is that perfect chef? Who is that perfect salesman? Who would you consider to be the perfect woman? Who would you consider to be the perfect man? Too difficult? Then try this: define the *characteristics* of the perfect woman or the perfect man. How tall are they? What level of education have they achieved? What job do they have? Do they even have jobs? How much money do they earn? Who or what do they look like physically? What is their body-type: skinny? Slim? Muscular? Rubenesque? Lovably-large? What is their innate intelligence: "genius?" "Normal?" Street-smart? What are their vices: do they smoke cigarettes? Do they drink alcohol? Do they even *have* any vices? Do they eat meat? Are they vegan? Are they married? Do they have children? If so, do they spank their children when the children misbehave, or do they give their child a time-out? Do they have a sense of humor? Are they serious and pensive? Is he a "mama's boy?" Is she a "daddy's little girl?" Have they previously been married? If so, how many exes would you be okay with them having? Do they have great hair, some hair, or no hair?

I am willing to bet my house that if these questions were asked of 10,000 different people I would receive no fewer than 10,000 different sets of characteristics that define the "perfect" man or woman. The reason is because perfection in a person is not universal, if it is at all achievable or even exists. In that sense, perfection is like "beauty": as "beauty is in the eye of the beholder," perfection is in the opinion of the *relevant receiver*.

The relevant receiver is the person or entity that has a direct and significant relationship to the matter at hand and is the intended audience of the matter. For example, if a man grows a full beard and his wife absolutely *loves* the way he looks with the beard (the matter at hand), but the haggard gas station attendant hates it, the man would be more inclined to keep the beard because his wife—the person to whom the man wants to appeal and whose opinion the man values—loves it. In this example, the man's wife is the relevant receiver because her opinion of the husband's handsomeness with the beard is the only opinion the man values (the *relevance*), and she is the person to whom the man is hoping to appeal by growing the beard; the wife's opinion of her husband's beard is the only opinion that matters in the determination of whether or not the beard stays.

So, when magazines publish their annual lists of "The Perfect Man" or "The Sexiest Person Alive," they believe that their intended audience of subscribers and supermarket-browsers (the *relevant receivers*) will agree with the magazines' choices. If the magazines' relevant receivers all agree that the magazines have, indeed, compiled a list of the "perfect" or "sexiest" people then, to the magazines, they have demonstrated that they and/or their readership have their fingers on the pulse of what people think, feel, and believe, which, in the end, will help sell more magazine subscriptions. Surely, the person or people the magazines and their readers have determined to be the #1 "perfect" or "sexiest" person on the lists should be widely-if-not-universally accepted by others as being the "perfect" and "sexiest" people as well, right? At a *minimum*, these #1 choices should also populate other magazines' lists of perfect, handsome, beautiful, and sexy people, too, shouldn't they? After all, who can deny "perfection"?

IN MAY 2013, CBS NEWS CONDUCTED A NATIONWIDE telephone poll of 1,200 randomly-selected adults nationwide for what they called "The *60 Minutes/Vanity Fair* Poll: The Perfect Man." The interviewees were asked: "Who is the perfect man? What qualities and characteristics make a good man or a man good?" During the interviews, one of the questions asked by the CBS News interviewers was: "If you could marry one of these television characters, who would you most likely choose?" Of the six actors presented, Patrick Dempsey, who portrays Dr. Derek Shepherd on the popular TV series *Grey's Anatomy*, won with a convincing 29% of the vote, with the next closest vote-getter, *Blue Bloods* actor Tom Selleck's Frank Reagan, receiving 13%. According to the *60 Minutes* poll, Patrick Dempsey would be considered the closest thing to "The Perfect Man"; or would that distinction go to his TV persona Dr. Derek Shepherd? In real-life, Patrick Dempsey is 5'10" and is once-divorced. Would, for instance, Women's National Basketball Association (WNBA) professional basketball star Elena Delle Donne (who is

6'5" tall) consider him to be her "perfect" man? Would a devout Christian who is steadfastly against divorce? And if the poll's respondents consider Dempsey's TV character Dr. Shepherd to be "The Perfect Man," on which qualities or characteristics did they base their judgment? On the show, Dr. Shepherd is often referred to as "McDreamy" and has received lots of press attention for his sex appeal. So, if we assume that Dempsey's/McDreamy's sex appeal was the basis for him garnering the most votes as *The Perfect Man*, then one would assume that Dempsey/McDreamy would also top other "Sexiest Man" lists, shouldn't he? After all, if these magazines believe that their polls are not totally worthless in the quest to identify what a "perfect man" is, then the top vote-getter should certainly find himself among the elite in other lists, shouldn't he?

Glamour Magazine conducted a poll of more than 95,000 people to develop their annual list of the 100 "*Glamour* Sexiest Men 2014." Guess who did not make the cut: Patrick Dempsey. How is that possible? Of the 100 men *Glamour* included in their "Sexiest Man" list, Patrick Dempsey didn't even get a sniff? Well, Patrick shouldn't feel that bad about his exclusion when he considers that the list also excluded every East and West Asian (none), Native American (zilch), Pacific Islander (zippo), and Latino (ninguno). I'm sure there's an Indian woman somewhere out there reading the article thinking, "What? In a country of 656 million men, there is not ONE Indian man who is sexier than *Theo Hutchcraft*?!"

And the picture is similarly muddled for women. In February 2013, *Men's Health* Magazine released its list of "The 100 Hottest Women of 2013." Unlike the CBS News poll and the *Glamour* survey, the *Men's Health* list was chosen by magazine editors—as though they somehow hold superior knowledge of what a "hot" woman really is. Wrote the editors: "Most of these women are very smart. Many are successful. All are smokin' hot—and that was our only criteria. Behold: This year's lust list."

As was the case with ethnic men in *Glamour's* "Sexiest Men 2014," the editors at *Men's Health* who chose the women for their "Hottest Women of 2013" list must not have believed there were any "smokin' hot" Asian women, because there were none to be found on the list. The woman the editors did, however, determine to be the "hottest" was ... Katy Perry. No, that's not a typo. *Katy Perry*! Just for the hell of it, I offered the following proposition to ten friends—friends of various ethnicities: You can have Katy Perry or any other woman you could think of, who would you choose? No surprise, all ten men chose someone else after quizzically wondering, "Katy *Perry*?" And I am willing to bet that there is a Chinese man waiting in line at the supermarket reading the *Men's Health* article thinking, "There are 645 million Chinese women and these editors couldn't find ONE Chinese woman sexier than *Azealia Banks* and *Kristen Wiig?!*"

Just as there are some men out there who would consider themselves physically perfect if, for instance, they looked like actor Patrick Dempsey, so too are there undoubtedly many women who would cut off a limb if they could look "hot" like Katy Perry or many of the other women listed in the *Men's Health* list of The 100 Hottest Women of 2013. Unfortunately for such dreamers, if they somehow actually morphed into Patrick Dempsey or Katy Perry, they would soon realize that being Patrick or Katy does not make them universally accepted as "perfect" or "hot," nor would it make them feel any more perfect than they had felt in their original skin. To believe otherwise is to believe that Patrick Dempsey, for instance, believes that he, himself, is without flaws—physical or otherwise—and that his performance as an actor has attained a level of excellence that cannot be exceeded. By all indications, Dempsey is very humble and grounded, so it would seem unlikely that he believes himself to be without physical flaws. But the minute he does start to believe it, he has only to review the pages of *Glamour's* Sexiest Men issue to learn otherwise.

And, yes, CBS also conducted "The *60 Minutes/Vanity Fair* Poll: The Perfect Woman." When male respondents were asked: "If you could marry one of these television characters, whom would you be most likely to choose?" The woman receiving the most votes (23%) was Kaley Cuoco-Sweeting who plays "Penny" on the TV show *The Big Bang Theory*. Upon further investigation, Cuoco-Sweeting didn't fare any better than did Patrick Dempsey when it came to "perfection" in other polls or in my informal "ten friends" test.

PLACE

Everyone at some point wishes that they could take that "perfect vacation" to some "perfect place." Although most people have or have had such a wish, the majority of us have never taken the time to actually sit down and determine the criteria that would define a vacation or a vacation destination as "perfect." *Conde Nast Traveler* is a magazine founded in 1987 to provide "Truth in Travel," with the goal of experiencing the world exactly as their readers do. Over the years, it has become one of—if not *the*—most trusted names in travel. In February 2014, *Conde Nast Traveler* published a list of the "31 Places to Have the Perfect Beach Vacation." Their #1 place was Jade Mountain, St. Lucia, of which they wrote "The black sand beach is great for snorkeling, but good luck leaving your private pool at your mountaintop suite ($1,125)." Okay, for starters, could Jade Mountain really be considered the #1 "perfect beach vacation" if—at a cost of $1,125 per night for the hotel room—it is only attainable by 5% of the population? From a cost standpoint, maybe they should have titled the article: "31 Places for *Millionaires* to Have the Perfect Beach Vacation."

Other than *Conde Nast Traveler*, what do others who have vacationed at the Jade Mountain Resort think of the place? A review of TripAdvisor, the world's largest travel site that reviews travel-related content and patrons' stays at swanky resorts like Jade Mountain, revealed that Jade Mountain is not perfect after all. In some reviews, feedback-providers described their experience as a "Most overrated hotel," "Not worth the money," and a "Mosquito Sanctuary." For these travelers, it appears Jade Mountain, St. Lucia is not a "perfect beach vacation" destination after all. This example of a "perfect" place supports the idea that what qualifies a place as being perfect, or the person who is vested with the authority and insight to sanctify a place as perfect, can only be determined by a relevant receiver.

THING

"Men grow cold as girls grow old, and we all lose our charms in the end. But square-cut or pear-shaped, these rocks don't lose their shape. Diamonds are a girl's best friend." So go the lyrics to the Jule Styne and Leo Robin-penned song "Diamonds are a Girl's Best Friend," most famously performed by Marilyn Monroe in the 1953 film *Gentlemen Prefer Blondes*. Listening to the song's lyrics and seeing how diamond rings have become the material representation of "I love you," one would get the impression that all women want diamond jewelry—and the more flawless the diamond, the better. A perfect-cut diamond? *Fuhgeddaboudit*.

Hearts on Fire, a global multi-channel manufacturer, marketer and designer of luxury branded diamonds and diamond jewelry, claims "The World's Most Perfectly Cut Diamond'" (they've even trademarked that claim). Hearts on Fire states that when you purchase a Hearts On Fire diamond, you are buying The Most Perfectly Cut Diamond In

The World®. They also state that less than one tenth of one percent of the world's diamonds can become a Hearts on Fire. One diamond offered by Hearts on Fire is the Dream Offset Signature Solitaire Engagement Ring. This ring was selected as a Hearts on Fire "Perfection Stylist's pick." Looking at the diamond's quality characteristics, you will find that the diamond is rated by Hearts on Fire as "Sensational," with *G-I* Color, and *VS1* to *SI1* Clarity. A diamond's authenticity—and, therefore, its quality and monetary value—is most commonly graded by the Gemological Institute of America's (GIA) "4Cs" grading system. The 4Cs provide a way to objectively compare and evaluate diamonds based on: Color [The GIA Color Scale extends from D (colorless) to Z (light yellow or brown), with colorless diamonds being of higher quality and thus, more precious]; Clarity [The GIA Clarity Scale includes eleven clarity grades ranging from Flawless to I3, diamonds with flaws or "Inclusions" ("I") are of lesser quality]; Cut [the GIA Cut Scale ranges from Excellent to Poor, with excellent-rated diamonds being the most scintillating]; and Carat weight [diamond size]. The Gemological Institute of America is the world's largest, most respected non-profit gemological knowledge source, and their diamond "D-to-Z" color-grading scale is the industry's most widely accepted grading system. Their 4Cs and International Diamond Grading System™ are the global standard. So surely, if a Hearts on Fire diamond rates a GIA "perfect" D (colorless)-Flawless (no Inclusions)-Excellent (brilliant cut), it would meet a globally-accepted standard for perfection, thus supporting their claim of "The World's Most Perfectly Cut Diamond˙."

Hearts on Fire shows that their Dream Offset Signature Solitaire Engagement Ring rated "G to I" in Color, and "VS1 to SI1" in Clarity. Applying this rating to the GIA scales, the Hearts on Fire diamond is, contrary to their trademark slogan, far from perfect.

If the company offering "The World's Most Perfectly Cut Diamond˙" cannot deliver a "perfect" diamond, then does a perfect diamond exist? Is perfection in a diamond even possible? Is unquestionable perfection in anyone or anything likely or even possible? This begs the question: what is *perfection*?

Perfection

Perfection suggests a state of flawlessness, without defects. People who desire perfection do so to overcome their perceived inadequacies, overcome their shortcomings, compensate for their deficiencies, and even because they fall prey to our culture's unachievable definitions of what the ideal or "perfect" person should be, do, have, or look like; and they do this so that all of their worldly problems will go away.

American logician Fredrick B. Fitch wrote in *The Monist* that the attribute of perfection can be defined in such a way as there can only be at most one perfect entity. This is done by defining something as perfect if it has a higher degree of perfection than anything else. He argues that the *attribute* perfection (the quality, character, characteristic, or property that affirms or denies something as being perfect) is perfect, but concedes that his argument assumes the perfection of perfection is "non-contingent" or, in other words, it assumes that the attribute perfection is an absolute—which, as I have argued, is one helluva flawed assumption. This raises the question: who defines the attributes of perfection and why should we concede that that person's definition is not in itself flawed and imperfect, thus rendering the thing that conforms to the person's perfection attribute imperfect itself? Robert Parker is arguably the world's most influential wine critic. *The Los Angeles Times* proclaimed "Parker is the most influential wine writer in the world today," and *Decanter* Magazine wrote "His influence is unparalleled in the history of wine journalism." Parker established a bi-monthly wine publication, *The Wine Advocate,* in which he rates wines on a 50-100 point scale. A wine with a rating of 96-100 is considered "extraordinary." Robert Parker has rated "perfect" (a score of 100 points) only seventy-six out of 220,000 wines tasted (3.5%). Surely, if *he* rates a wine as perfect it must be unparalleled in its category and the "very best produced of their type," right? One wine which Parker rated a perfect 100/100 was the 1945 Baron Philippe de Rothschild Chateau Mouton Rothschild, Pauillac, France with an average selling price of $15,692. However, *Wine Spectator* Magazine rated the wine 94/100 and French Wine Critic Jean-Marc Quarin, publisher of *Carnets de Degustations* wine newsletter, rated the wine 93/100—still "excellent" but not perfect. Parker himself implies that a wine's perfection is subjective and based on the judgment of the taster (the relevant receiver) when he writes "However, there can never be any substitute for your own palate nor any better education than tasting the wine yourself."

Literary and art critic Lucien Rudrauf, in *The Journal of Aesthetics and Art Criticism* described perfection as a "...bewildering concept, unintelligible to common sense...," a description that I embrace wholeheartedly. To be perfect implies a condition whereby your action or performance attains a level of excellence that cannot be exceeded. Can you think of anything that is without defects? Can you think of any person's skill set, performance, or level of accomplishment that cannot or will not ever be exceeded? Some would argue, for example, that professional basketball player Wilt Chamberlain's March 2, 1962 feat of scoring 100 points in a professional basketball game will never be broken. The closest anyone has come to threatening that record was Los Angeles Lakers' player Kobe Bryant, who scored 81 points back in 2006—only 19 points shy of tying the record. Based on Bryant's accomplishment, it is not inconceivable that Wilt Chamberlain's record will eventually be broken. But, even if the scoring record is never broken, was Chamberlain's play that March night "a level of excellence that cannot be exceeded?" Scoring 100 points in a game is not "perfection," but scoring 100 points while not missing any shots, not allowing your opponent (whom Wilt was guarding in the game) to score any points, and grabbing every rebound possible would be. It would be a level of excellence that could "not be exceeded." Against these measures of perfection, how did Wilt fare? According to the National Basketball Association's box score from that game, Wilt made only 57% of his 63 shots from the field, and he made 88% of his 32 free throws; his opponent scored 7 points. Based on the evidence, even records that might stand the test of time were not necessarily "perfect" performances.

In May 2014, Sotheby's, most widely known as one of the premier auction houses in the world, auctioned and sold a "Very Important Diamond" for $6,246,702. The round brilliant diamond weighed 25.32 carats, and was authenticated by the GIA, which stated "… the diamond is D Colour, Type IIa, Internally Flawless, Excellent Cut, Excellent Polish, Excellent Symmetry." This diamond was as perfect a diamond as you will ever find. Yet, even this "Very Important Diamond" was not perfect—without flaws. The diamond's GIA-rated Clarity was "*Internally* Flawless," which is one level short of the highest "Flawless" rating. And who's to say that the GIA's rating system is flawless? This raises the question: Can a *thing* like a diamond be perfect in an *absolute* sense or does "perfection" take into consideration more than just scores on a grading scale? In other words, is a diamond's perfection *relative*? This introduces the doctrines of absolutism and relativism.

Absolutism is the doctrine that reality is unitary, unchanging, and universal, and not relative to individual or social differences. In other words, if something is perfect, then that thing or person is perfect regardless of what someone may think. On the other hand, *relativism* is the doctrine that knowledge, truth, and morality exist in a cultural, societal, or historical context, and are not absolute. In other words, whether something or someone is perfect depends on many factors; it is not cast in stone. Absolutists would argue that, in an absolute sense, for instance, puncturing your skin with a sewing needle hurts, regardless of who you are. If you asked 100 people what it would feel like if you were to stick a needle in their back, every rational person would say the needle would *hurt*. Why? Because our experience being stuck by needles tells us that it results in a painful feeling under any condition. In a relative sense, however, there are certain cases where sticking a needle into a person's back would bring pleasure—think acupuncture—or no feeling at all, as in the case of people who suffer from a condition such as Congenital Insensitivity to Pain with Anhidrosis. So even pain, relativists would argue, is not an absolute.

The discussion of whether any person, place, or thing is or can be *absolutely* perfect raises the question about whether a person's, place's, or thing's perfection is, therefore, *objective,* or is it relative and *subjective* (based on a person's opinion). For a person's perfection, for instance, to be objective means that the determination of that person's perfection cannot be influenced by personal feelings, interpretations, or prejudice; it is based on unbiased facts. If objective, the person's perfection should exist independent of thought or an observer as being reality. Is there *anything* that has been deemed perfect by a human being that is agreed by all to be perfect, regardless of what other people think about it? A diamond? Kaley Cuoco-Sweeting? Jade Mountain Resort? If so, who determines the objective perfection of a person, place, or thing?

The view of "objectivism" offered by Richard J. Bernstein in his book *Beyond Objectivism and Relativism* suggests there must be an appellate authority to decide on such matters as "perfection":

> "… the basic conviction that there is or must be some permanent, ahistorical matrix or framework to which we can ultimately appeal in determining the nature of rationality, knowledge, truth, reality, goodness, or rightness …"

Must we? For fear of *skepticism*? Is Bernstein suggesting that, if there is a dispute over whether or not the Jade Mountain Resort is a perfect vacation destination, there should be a *perfection judge* to offer the final verdict? Then who would that "perfection judge" be, and what would qualify the person for such a role?

I believe that perfection—just as "beauty" and "tastiness" and "good-smelling"—is an *aesthetic judgment*. It is a feeling; it is a perception. It is perceived by a person's senses or mind.

In his 1963 paper *Objectivism and Aesthetics*, Australian philosopher H. J. McCloskey argued that we can regard aesthetic judgments as being in the sphere of truth and falsity, because genuine disagreements may arise concerning them. He wrote that "… although aesthetic judgments are judgments that are in the sphere of truth and falsity, they rest on *perceptions* that are in many ways akin to those of the senses…" He states that because aesthetic judgments involve such perceptions, few people, if any, could be an authority on that which is being perceived. However, just because we regard aesthetic judgments as being in the sphere of truth and falsity, we should not make the mistake of conceding that such aesthetic judgments are true or false. For example, we should not concede that the judgment "Patrick Dempsey is perfect" is true, correct, or right irrespective of who makes the assertion—that is, of who is the observer. This supports my previously offered opinion that perfection, like beauty, is the opinion of the relevant receiver—the *observer*. With this opinion, it appears that even the Gemological Institute of America—the global authority on determining whether or not a diamond is "perfect" according to their grading system—would agree.

When it comes to the perfection of a diamond, even the GIA says that "numbers alone can't describe a diamond's mysterious and captivating beauty—for that, you'll have to visit your local jeweler to see one for yourself," which implies that a diamond's beauty and perfection is ultimately an *aesthetic judgment* of the relevant receiver; it is subjective.

Conflict diamonds (also called "blood diamonds") are diamonds sold to fund armed conflict and civil war. Profits from the trade in conflict diamonds, worth billions of dollars, are used by warlords and rebels to buy arms for fighting wars in Angola, the Democratic Republic of Congo, and Sierra Leone; wars that have cost an estimated 3.7 million lives. Say, for instance, a woman who is involved in the international boycott of diamonds mined in Zimbabwe—and who therefore has an unfavorable opinion of diamonds as a currency that supports genocide—is presented with Sotheby's "Very Important Diamond." Would the woman consider the diamond to be "perfect" or even beautiful? Would she care that the diamond is highly rated by the GIA? Would she care that the diamond cost more than $6M dollars? No. And the fact that the ring cost so much money would probably piss her off even more, as she drew a connection between the diamond's price and the number of lives it could have cost, even if the Sotheby's diamond was actually conflict-free.

So, while it is possible a diamond could technically meet the GIA standard for being a "perfect" diamond, from a practical standpoint, a diamond's perfection is a function of both the diamond's GIA rating and the relevant receiver's (the person for whom the diamond is being acquired) perception of the diamond as "perfect" for her or him based on what they value and what their eye responds to.

But surely, there must be *something* that is indisputably perfect, mustn't there?

What about "God"?

Some people, especially religious believers, will argue that the only perfect thing is God. While this may be open to debate, as I will show in subsequent paragraphs, something we know for sure, however, is that the Christian Bible acknowledges that *people* are *imperfect*:

> *Proverbs* 26:12
> Do you see a man who is wise in his own eyes?
> There is more hope for a fool than for him.

Popular American Pastor Rick Warren appears to agree. On his website rickwarren.org, he wrote that "We are not perfect; God is perfect. We are flawed; God is flawless." His statement is consistent with what is written in passage 2 Samuel 22:31 of the Christian Holy Bible:

> As for God, his way is perfect:
> The Lord's word is flawless;
> he shields all who take refuge in him.

If true—and I would imagine that all Christians believe it to be so—then we will have identified that one "perfect" thing: the Christian God. But, are there multiple gods or is the Christian God the same God worshiped in other religions, such as Islam, Buddhism, Judaism, Confucianism, Yoruba, and Daoism? In his book, *God is Not One: The Eight Rival Religions That Run the World, New York Times* bestselling author and religion scholar Stephen Prothero argues that persistent attempts to portray all religions as different paths to the same God overlook the distinct problem that each tradition seeks to solve.

The "same God" question (in other words, whether or not

all religions worship the same God) is one that theologians have explored for centuries with no definitive answer. But, what if Jesus Christ is God, as many Christians believe? If so, one can make the case that at least the Christian God and the Islamic God ("Allah") are likely not the same because their teachings and texts are incompatible. Both religions would argue that *their* version of the scripture is correct and *their* God is the one perfect God.

In this example, either one religion's version of a perfect God is correct and the other is wrong, or both are wrong. Since perfection means that nothing can be equal to or more perfect than that which is considered perfect, there can only be one perfect thing, or one perfect God—if belief in a god's perfection is absolute. This leaves room for other religions to make the case for why the other rival religions' Gods are not the "true" God and, therefore, cannot be perfect because *their* God is the only true God, the *only* perfect thing. And if they all believe that their Gods are perfect—which they do—then, by extension of the preceding logic, it is possible that none of their Gods are "perfect."

The various religions' beliefs in the truth and perfection of their Gods are a reflection of their *faith*. Faith is belief with strong conviction; firm belief in something for which there may be no tangible proof. Because people's belief that their God is the one true, perfect God is based on faith—belief in something with no proof—the probability that they are correct in their assertion is less than 100%, which means that it is possible the various religions could be mistaken about the perfection of their Gods. In other words, it is possible that all of the various religions' Gods are imperfect.

There are, however, some people of faith who believe that even their own God is likely to not be perfect. Yoram Hazony, an Israeli philosopher, Orthodox Jew, and the author of *The Philosophy of Hebrew Scripture* disagrees with theists who believe that God is all-powerful, all-knowing, immutable, and perfectly good. He believes that the attempt to think of God as a perfect being is misguided. As he wrote in the opinion pages of the *New York Times:*

> "… it seems unlikely that God can be both perfectly powerful and perfectly good if the world is filled (as it obviously is) with instances of terrible injustice. … The God of Hebrew Scripture is not depicted as immutable, but repeatedly changes his mind about things (for example, he regrets having made man). He is not all-knowing, since he's repeatedly surprised by things (like the Israelites abandoning him for a statue of a cow). He is not perfectly powerful either, in that he famously cannot control Israel and get its people to do what he wants. And so on."

While various religions may not agree on whether they all worship the same God or if their God is the one true, perfect God, there is another community of people who most certainly do not believe *any* of the gods are perfect: atheists.

Atheists deny or disbelieve the existence of a supreme being; many argue that "agnostics"—people who are uncertain
about whether or not there is a God—are also atheists since
they do not certainly believe there is a God. A 2012 survey
conducted by the Pew Research Center for the People &
the Press found that 19 million people in the U.S. *admit*
to being either atheist or agnostic, and 19.6% (65 million
people) are non-believers and non-religious. I say "admit"
to being either atheist or agnostic, because atheists believe
the number to be much higher due to the belief that a significant number of non-believers are reluctant to admit it
in a survey or publicly. I have seen estimates that show the
percentage of American non-believers to be much higher.
Adherents.com (a collection of more than 43,870 religion
statistics and religious geography citations used by researchers) published data that show 850 million people globally
who identify as either secular, nonreligious, agnostic, or
atheist. Whatever the number, the message is clear: There
are millions of people across the U.S. and around the world
who disagree that there is such a thing as a "perfect" God.
So, if all religions believe their God is perfect, some religious
people doubt the perfection of their God, and millions of
other people do not believe that there is a perfect God at all,
then, as I have pointed out throughout this book, nothing
is universally agreed to be perfect. Perfection, however it is
defined, is subjective in the opinion of the relevant receiver.

2

"Your Perfection"

THE QUIET REVERIE OF PAT THE FARM FRESH EGG

Pat, the egg—yes, *that* kind of egg, the kind you eat—had a decision to make: to hang around on the farm for an additional three weeks to hatch into a chick, or to board a pickup truck heading for the local farmer's market to be sold to some health-conscious shopper looking for farm-fresh eggs. In the world of chickens and eggs, this is not an easy decision to make because, as Pat understood, there are pros and cons to both options.

If Pat decided to be incubated so he/she could hatch into a chick, once hatched, Pat's fate would largely be influenced by whether it hatched into a male chick or a female chick. If Pat hatched into a female (or hen), she could grow up to be an Orpington broody hen, just like her mom, and would be destined to a life of laying eggs for commercial sale. If Pat hatched into a male (a rooster), he could grow up to be a proud broiler chicken just like his dad, go into the family business, and be sold for the table where—if he is lucky—he might be roasted at the local supermarket and sold to some appreciative family for $5.99.

The challenge for Pat when deciding whether or not to get hatched was that there was no way to tell in advance if the egg would hatch into a female chick or a male chick (excluding, perhaps, intra-ova DNA testing); eggs will generally hatch out in a 50:50 gender mix, so Pat's fate, if it hatched, would basically be determined by a coin-toss. To make matters worse, Pat feared, if it hatched in a hatchery that wanted only females for laying eggs and Pat hatched into a male, Pat would be unwanted and in all likelihood immediately killed to reduce costs to the breeder. Yikes! But, there was another option: Pat could decide to go unhatched and remain an egg. As an egg, Pat would not only avoid the potential risks associated with hatching, but it could also do what it and other farm-fresh eggs dreamed about from the time they were oocytes: join a professional baking-ingredient team, be made into a "perfect" cupcake, and compete in and win the National Cupcake Championships. Sure, Pat could have been happy joining the family business as a chicken—assuming he hatched into one—but Pat wanted more. He wanted to be part of a cupcake, something kids of all races, colors, and creeds coveted more than even chicken nuggets.

Pat wasn't just any old egg; it was a prized, farm-fresh large egg, the kind that professional bakers covet most. The reason is that most baking recipes call for about 6 1/2 tablespoons of liquid egg—the amount contained in one large egg. Extra-large and jumbo eggs add far more liquid than successful baking recipes call for, and small & medium eggs do not provide enough. When it comes to professional baking and the use of eggs, size matters.

And so it was decided: Pat would remain an egg and go off to the farmer's market to be sold. While resting in the market waiting to be sold, Pat met several other foods and they all became quick friends. Pat met some other large eggs, some organic all-purpose flour, baking powder, sea salt, cane sugar, vanilla beans, and in the dairy section, he became acquainted with fresh churned butter and milk. These "Ingredients," as they called themselves, talked for hours on end about being sold to a pastry chef, forming a team, and joining forces to be developed into something perfect—a perfect cupcake. Sure, for Pat, there was dignity in being scrambled, poached, or fried and eaten by some egg-loving kid who could benefit from the nutrients that Pat provided. But, how many eggs could say that they were part of something "perfect?" As luck would have it, Pat and the other Ingredients were purchased by a professional pastry chef who masterfully combined the Ingredients into what they believed was a perfect cupcake.

It was now September, and Pat's perfect cupcake was headed off to participate in the National Cupcake Week festivities. A win would not only earn the pastry chef a trophy and accolades for an outstanding culinary performance, it would also mean the cupcake, itself—and by association, the Ingredients—were seen by the judges and many of the spectators as something special. People would applaud them; fans would line up to photograph them; and they would receive the most flattering compliment of all—kids would want to eat them! For the Ingredients, and to Pat the egg in particular, a win at the National Cupcake Championships would be validation that they had, indeed, produced a perfect cupcake. It would solidify their value and give them a sense of worth. Or would it?

"And the winner is …" boomed the voice over the loudspeakers at the National Cupcake Week festivities. No. Pat the egg's cupcake did not win the Championship. But, to the

surprise of some of the other Ingredients, Pat was not disappointed. Sure, Pat thought, it would have been nice to win so
that everyone's collective effort would have been recognized
publicly, but even in defeat, Pat the egg felt proud—proud,
because it had done its best to contribute to the cupcake's
outcome. Pat had done its best and added structure, leaven-
ing, color, and flavor to the cupcake. It worked in harmony
with the flour to provide the cupcake's height and texture.
And when Pat's whites were whipped, it helped the cupcake
to rise to its final beauty. In Pat's opinion, the cupcake was
"perfect."

Pat and the other Ingredients did not believe that the
judges' collective opinion of a cupcake's perfection was any
more valid than their own. In fact, since the cupcakes defined "perfection" based on their own standards, expectations, and purpose, to them, theirs was the only definition
of perfection that mattered.

Pat the egg did not believe that a determination of perfection could be made by imperfect human beings based
on imperfect senses required to determine a cupcake's "perfection": taste, smell, sight, and touch. A catfish has about
20,000 taste buds in its mouth, or about twice as many as a
human does. But, the catfish has an additional 180,000 taste
buds on the outside of his body, which means that all in all
it has 20 times as many taste buds as humans do, meaning
our human sense of taste is not perfect. So, is anyone's pal-
ate so perfectly-discriminating that one can taste the exact
amount of vanilla that was added to the cupcake's batter and

distributed into each cupcake?

Eagles and other birds of prey can see four to five times farther than the average human can, meaning they have 20/5 or 20/4 vision under ideal viewing conditions; humans—at best—have 20/20 vision, meaning our vision is far from perfect. So did the judges have perfect eyesight to be able to detect all the cupcakes' visual nuances?

Researchers have estimated that a bloodhound's nose has approximately 230 million olfactory cells, or "scent receptors"—40 times the number found in humans. And since smell impacts our tasting abilities, if humans have an imperfect or flawed sense of smell and taste, could the judges have been capable of rendering a verdict on the perfection of anything edible, including a cupcake?

Pat was not disappointed, because Pat understood that the judges' opinion was just that—their opinion. It was an opinion based on their *aesthetic judgment*, a judgment influenced by their imperfect senses of taste, smell, touch, and sight. To Pat, the importance of the judges' opinion was insignificant compared to Pat's (and the Ingredients') opinion of perfection in the outcome of their combined efforts—the cupcake. Pat was truly satisfied with having given the most of itself; having put forth the best effort it could toward *becoming the best it could become* which, in Pat's opinion, was an ingredient in the absolute best cupcake that the Ingredients could possibly produce. That, Pat realized, was its "perfection."

What is Your Perfection?

What is *your* perfection? If a genie popped out of a magic lamp and told you that he would grant you the wish to make you "perfect," but in order for the genie to deliver on the wish, he would need to know how you wanted to be. What would you tell him is your version of perfection? To be rich? What exactly is "rich" to you? To have $5 million in the bank? Why not $50 million? Is it to be 6-feet tall? Why is that height perfect? Why not 6'2"? Is it to be a size 4? Why not a size 2? Is your perfection to look like Patrick Dempsey? Why not look like Zac Efron, Boris Kodjoe, Enrique Iglesias, Rock Hudson, or Billy Dee Williams in his prime? Is your perfection to look like Kaley Cuoco-Sweeting ? Why not Julia Ling or Jude Schimmel? Is it to be as successful in your field of work as former Apple CEO Steve Jobs was in his? Why not Warren Buffett or IBM CEO Ginni Rometty? Is your perfection to be as "intelligent" as Terence Tao? Why not Emilie Chatelet (considered by some to be the smartest women ever) or Stephen Hawking? *How would you define your perfection?*

The major challenge with defining perfection in this sense is exactly that: defining perfection. If you have never considered it, when you do, you will find—as I have—that it is difficult if not impossible. Give it a try. Using the table below, define "your perfection determinant" (the characteristic that would contribute to your perfection) for each "attribute."

Attribute	Your Perfection Determinant
Education	(example: college degree)
Physical condition	
Height	
Weight	
Physical build	
Body type	
Body characteristic 1	
Body characteristic 2	
Body characteristic 3	
Career / occupation	
Annual income	
Expertise	
Skill mastered 1	
Skill mastered 2	
Skill mastered 3	
Family situation	
Relationship status	
Children's adeptness	
Facial features resembling (whom)	
Age	
Hair	
Shoe size	
Sexual "prowess"	
House	
Car	
Friendships	
Community support	
Level of fame and notoriety	
Popularity level	
"Q" rating (likability)	
Intelligence Quotient (I.Q.)	
Spirituality	
Philanthropy / charity	
Infinite other options	

Let's assume that for each of the 33 Attributes listed in the table (excluding the final category, "Infinite Other Options"), there is an average of 20 Perfection Determinants that you could choose from or decide on. For example, for the attribute "House," there could be an A-frame, Addison house, American Colonial, Georgian Colonial, Spanish Colonial, Bungalow, Cape Cod, Castle, Cottage, Farmhouse, Georgian House, Laneway house, Link-detached, Log cabin, Manor house, Mansion, Pre-fabricated house, Single-family detached home, Victorian house, and/or Villa. Given the number of perfection attributes and the associated number of Perfection Determinants in this table, the total number of Perfection Determinants would be 8 tredecillion:

8,689,934,600,000,000,000,000,000,000,000,000,000,000,000

In other words, the chances of another person selecting the exact same Perfection Determinants for each Attribute you selected is … highly unlikely, which means that no one else would agree with your version of perfection. Put more simply, if the genie granted your wish and made you perfect based on your determination of perfection, no one else would think that you were perfect. To make matters worse, in reality, we know that the number of potential perfection attributes that a person can choose from is far greater than the number included in the table above, and the possible number of Perfection Determinants for each attribute is greater, too, meaning that the chances of another human being defining perfection in the same way as you define it is practically impossible. If that is the case, then there can be no absolute standard of perfection except for one: the one you define for yourself; "your perfection."

The number of possible definitions of perfection is infinite, and I believe perfection is therefore like infinity: we all get the idea, but in actuality, it is unreachable.

Why do we want to be perfect anyway?

In Neil Burger's 2011 film *Limitless*, Eddie Morra (played by Bradley Cooper) is an unsuccessful writer whose life is transformed by a top-secret drug that allows him "to become a perfect version of himself." The drug unlocked 100% of his brain giving him full mental capacity, far greater than the 20% of the brain available to us mere mortals. He was suddenly able to speak other languages; he became a math whiz; he became cultured; he wrote a book in 4 days (which, of course, became a best seller); and he became rich & famous. He became his own ideal of "perfect." Life was great. In one scene, while Morra contemplated the wonderful benefits of taking the unknown pill without knowing its long-term side-effects, he asks: "Would you risk it?"

Well, would you? Would you take such a pill if taking the pill allowed you to achieve perfection—as you define it—for a finite period? If you ask people whether or not they would like to be perfect or achieve perfection in some measure, characteristic, condition, or activity, almost all of them would say "Yes;" they would want to be Eddie Morra. When asked why, the reasons range from "a better life" to "happiness." But, I believe that people who desire perfection do so on a more psychological level than a materialistic one. I believe people simply want to be "their best selves possible" by maximizing their potential and achieving what Abraham Maslow called *Self-Actualization.*

Self-Actualization

In his 1943 paper, *A Theory of Human Motivation*, and his later book, *Motivation and Personality*, psychologist Abraham Maslow proposed that all human behavior is motivated by need; specifically, a hierarchy of needs. He referred to it as a hierarchy—often depicted as a pyramid—because our primary, basic needs (such as food or shelter) must be satisfied before we can move on to satisfying higher-level needs, such as companionship. Maslow believed that needs create instinctual behaviors in people which motivate us to behave in ways that satisfy these needs.

**An Interpretation of
Maslow's Hierarchy of Needs**

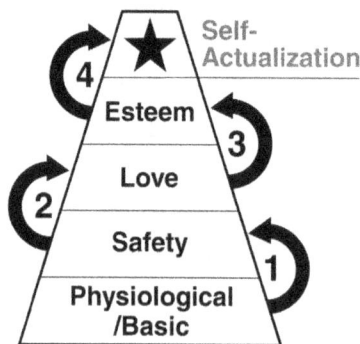

According to Maslow, the appearance of one need is contingent upon the prior satisfaction of another, lower-level need. Basic physiological needs are considered a greater priority than higher needs on the pyramid. They must be met before the person can move up the hierarchy. In other words, a person who is starving will not concentrate on building self-esteem.

Maslow's original theory consisted of five needs. The first are physical needs; the instinctive basic needs necessary for survival, which include food, water, oxygen, and sleep. Until these needs are met, all other needs are secondary. Once basic needs are met, man can turn his attention to safety and security. To early man, that would have been a cave and a fire to keep away predators. To modern man, this may refer to employment, shelter, medical care, and a safe environment in which to live. The next level up the hierarchy encompasses social, or emotional needs, such as friendship, a sense of belonging, romantic love, and general affection. If we can't find companionship in other people, we'll seek it out in community groups, religions, and even our pets. Once we are secure in our survival needs and safety and personal relationships, self-esteem becomes important. This manifests as a desire for external recognition and individual accomplishment. We don't need it to survive, but we do need it to feel good about ourselves. This need for esteem leads directly to the top of the pyramid: self-actualization. This is when an individual focuses on personal growth and is less concerned about other people's opinions. The goal is to reach and fulfill their own potential. Maslow defined self-actualization as the process of personal development to achieve and maximize one's potential.

Maslow deemed the first four levels as "deficiency" needs, or D-needs, because they are caused by deprivation. He labeled self-actualization as a "being" need, or B-need, because it wasn't prompted by a lack of something, but by a desire for personal growth. Self-actualization is person-specific, as is perfection. Maslow points out that, for one person, it could be a desire to be an outstanding parent; for another, it could be to express oneself through arts or science. It must be defined by the person for the person.

So, based on Maslow's *Theory of Human Motivation*, when we wish for financial wealth, we are probably trying to satisfy the need for security; when we wish for "beauty," we are probably trying to satisfy the needs for love and esteem; when we wish for super-intelligence or to be great in our fields of interest, we are probably trying to satisfy the need for esteem, toward self-actualization. And when we wish for "perfection," we are probably trying to be our best possible self, satisfying all of the "deficiency" needs (D-needs), as well as the "being" needs (B-needs).

Types of Needs

Physiological Needs	Examples
The basic needs, or physiological drives, that are considered the starting point for motivation. Until these needs are satisfied, human beings cannot function optimally (if at all).	Food, Shelter, Water, Sleep, and Oxygen

Safety Needs	Examples
People have a need to feel safe and free from danger and harm. We have a desire to live in an orderly, predictable, and organized world in which unexpected, unmanageable, or dangerous things do not take place. And, if they do, we have the ability to protect ourselves.	Security, Stability, Order, and Physical Safety

Love Needs	Examples
If both physiological and safety needs are fairly well-gratified, then the needs for love, affection and a sense of belonging will emerge. A person will noticeably feel the absence of friends, or a partner, or a spouse, or children. She will hunger for affectionate relationships with people in general, namely, for a place in a group, and she will strive with great intensity to achieve this goal. The person will want to attain such a position more than anything else in the world and may even forget that once, when she was hungry, she didn't give love and affection the slightest thought.	Affection, Identification, and Companionship

Esteem Needs	Examples
The satisfaction of the self-esteem need leads to feelings of self-confidence, worth, strength, adequacy, and the capability to be useful and necessary in the world. But, the thwarting of these needs produces feelings of inferiority, weakness, and helplessness.	Self-respect, Prestige, Success, and the Respect of others

Self-Actualization Need	Examples
Even if all other needs are satisfied, we may still often (if not always) expect that a new discontent and restlessness will soon develop, unless the individual is doing what he or she was meant to do. To ultimately be happy, a musician must make music; an artist must paint; and a poet must write. What a man can be, he must be. This need is called self-actualization.	Self-fulfillment, Understanding, and Achieving one's own potential

Though the pursuit of Self-Actualization is a reasonable theory for why people desire perfection, I sincerely doubt that, if asked about their perfection desire, anyone would offer that as an explanation. I previously wrote that if you ask people whether or not they would like to be perfect or achieve perfection in some measure, characteristic, condition, or activity, almost all of them would say "Yes." And when asked "Why," the reasons would range from "a better life" to "happiness."

My question to you is this: Why do you believe that if you acquired all the Perfection Determinants defined in the Attribute Table from the above section, you would be perfect? Why do you believe life would be "better" or you would feel "content" or you would be "happy"? Respondents often say that if they achieved perfection, then contentment and happiness would come because they would be free from worry; they wouldn't have to struggle; they would find love; and they would be valued in the world.

The question: "Why do you believe that if you acquired all the attributes defined in the above table you would be perfect?" is the same as asking "Why do you *want* to be perfect?" If your responses to either question are similar to the aforementioned, then *why* do you believe achieving perfection will make life better, make you content, or make you happy? And if perfection is unattainable, then are you resigned to never achieving contentment, happiness, and a sense of self-worth? Are you resigned to leading a miserable life if you cannot achieve "perfection?"

The Elusiveness of Perfection

In 2012, the *Daily Mail* published an article titled "The perfect man DOES exist ... in fact there are FIVE of them out there!" citing research "… proving that there is indeed a 'perfect man' for every stage in a woman's life." The article presented the characteristics that women in different age ranges look for in a partner; certain characteristics make a perfect man for each age in a woman's life. Characteristics varied somewhat by age (e.g. women between the ages of 25-34 preferred different characteristics in a perfect man than did women in the 55+ category). However, I have condensed all characteristics into one list below.

- A man they can show off to their friends;
- A six-pack (defined abdominal muscles);
- Shared tastes in music, films and books;
- Physical attraction;
- Sexual compatibility;
- Ambition;
- Social graces;
- Security;
- A high income;
- Intelligence and shared values.

So, men, if you provided the magic genie with this list in your quest to become that perfect guy, the genie—with a quizzical look of exasperation on his blue face—would probably say "Okay, let's review each characteristic you provided me with so that I can get a better idea of what I am supposed to turn you into."

Characteristic	The Genie's Remarks
A man they can show off to their friends	"What does *that* mean? What about you do they want to show off? Your looks? Your attire? Your knowledge? Your car? What? Are they so insecure that they need a man's … looks … to score kudos from their judgmental friends?"

Characteristic	The Genie's Remarks
A six-pack (defined abdominal muscled)	"Check."
Shared tastes in music, films and books	"What does *that* mean? Are you supposed to like the same music, movies, and books that *she* likes? That's awfully selfish, isn't it? Why does that matter? What—will she dump you if you didn't think 'The Notebook' was Oscar-worthy and *she* did?"
Physical attraction	"What does *that* mean? Should she be physically attracted to your face? Your body? Or, regardless of how you look, should she just want to bed you because she finds you sexy? What are you supposed to look like? Does she want you to look like Patrick Dempsey—the same guy who couldn't crack the top-100 in *Glamour* Magazine's list of the Sexiest Men 2014—or some other ideal that, to others, would be considered hideous?"
Sexual compatibility	"What does *that* mean? Does she mean a certain endowment? Does it mean that if she enjoys S&M pornography you should, too? Does it mean that she will have sex with you just to see if you are ... 'compatible' ... and, if you are not, she will dump you? I need more specifics!"
Ambition	"What does *that* mean? Does it mean that she wants you to play company politics to get that promotion? Does it mean that if you are a painter you've got no shot? Does it mean that you should never be satisfied with your current station in life—even if your current station is pretty darn good? What does she want?"

Characteristic	The Genie's Remarks
Social graces	"What does *that* mean? When out having dinner—especially with guests—you must eat European style? You must have attended finishing school or charm school? You must always be polite in social settings, even to a**holes?" What exactly are the criteria?"
Security (feels secure when with you)	"What does *that* mean? Does she want you to become a 7th Dan Black Belt in karate? Does she want you to pack heat when she's with you? Does she want you to constantly tell her 'You're the only one'? What will make her feel "secure" and why is she so insecure in the first place?"
A high income	"What does *that* mean? Income levels are relative. If the women lived in the underbelly of Detroit, Michigan, subsisting on $8,000 per year, she would think a man is rich if he even earned the U.S. median annual household income of $51,939, while Christy Walton (the widow of Wal-Mart's John Walton) would consider Donald Trump to be broke."
Intelligence and shared values	"What does *that* mean? What does she mean by 'intelligence'? Is she talking about your score on an I.Q. test or is she talking about your ability to survive alone, unassisted for six months during an Australian Aboriginal Walkabout? And does she really mean *shared* values or does she mean you should have *her* values? That's awfully selfish, isn't it? What in the world does she mean?!"

As the genie's interrogation illustrates, even if women provided you with a list of what they considered to be the characteristics of a perfect man (save for six-pack abs), it would still be ambiguous at best and impossible to articulate at worst, leaving you just as you are today: "perfect" in someone's opinion, even if not your own.

And, women, it doesn't get any easier for the magic genie when it comes to making you the perfect woman. In 2012, *Huffington Post* published an article titled "The 5 Things Successful Men Notice First in a Woman." The article described five of the most important qualities successful men notice first when considering dating a woman and assessing the possibility of a future with her.

1. Verbal and written communication;

2. Posture;

3. The way a woman carries herself when she walks, or her gait;

4. A Sense of self (the extent of their knowledge when it came to current events, politics and culture);

5. Their hair (Keeping hair a natural hue and focusing on how healthy it looks greatly ups your chances).

Upon reading this list, I'm sure the genie yelled: "What?! I have to throw the bulls—t flag on this one! Are they kidding me?!" The cause for the genie's consternation, I am sure, is the disingenuity of the "successful" men's responses to the questions. "Verbal and written communication" #1? Uh … yeah, sure.

Characteristic	The Genie's Remarks
Verbal and written communication	"What?! Are they looking for a soul mate or someone to write their term papers? Does it simply mean that the woman need only know how to speak and write, or are the men expecting Hortensia? Will the men, at some point, give the women the 'Critical Reading' section of the SAT exam to complete—and decide whether or not to keep her based on her score?"
Posture	"What!? Is that man-code for 'big breasts' or are the men looking for West Point graduates and ballerinas, as opposed to hard-working mothers?"
The way a woman carries herself when she walks, or her gait	"What does *that* mean? The way she 'carries herself when she walks'? I bet the men themselves don't even know what that means. Her 'gait?' Do they want a spouse or Secretariat?"
A Sense of self (the extent of their knowledge when it came to current events, politics and culture)	"What the hell does *that* mean? Does it mean that men want a woman who is a Public Broadcasting Services (PBS) News anchorwoman? I'm starting to see a pattern here with men: based on their 'likes,' they seem hell-bent on testing women's knowledge."
Their hair (Keeping hair a natural color and focusing on how healthy it looks greatly ups your chances)	"Ha, ha, ha, ha, ha!! I understand what men are saying, but reading it ('natural hue'? 'Greatly ups your chances'?) is pretty funny. Check."

To humor myself—and to make sure that I wasn't in the *Twilight Zone*, I asked the same ten friends—the friends I had previously polled about Katy Perry—the same *Huffington Post* question: "List the most important qualities you notice first when considering dating a woman and assessing the possibility of a future with her." While I will acknowledge that polling ten friends & colleagues does not a scientific study make, I figured that, if nothing else, their answers should be entertaining. What surprised me about the answers these ten smart, talented, responsible, successful, middle-aged men gave was not that the answers differed so greatly from the *Huffington Post* survey responses (which they did), but that their answers were more consistent with the characteristics I used to hear wantonly thrown around at college fraternity parties. Go figure. Anyway, the top five answers given by the ten respondents—answers which were pretty consistent to a man—are provided below.

1. The woman's face;

2. The woman's genuineness (not putting on a facade, being "down to earth" and fun);

3. The woman's style (neatness, style of dress, and the *hands-hair-feet* triumvirate);

4. The woman's body (figure, shape, proportions, and attributes);

5. The woman's intelligence (not necessarily formal education, including common sense).

The point is this: Whether a stranger provided you with a list of characteristics that supposedly define the perfect person or if you developed your own list of perfection attributes, even if you could realize those characteristics, you would still not achieve perfection. The reason is perfection is subjective and is influenced by, among other things, the times in which a person lives—meaning that it is also *relative* and not absolute. For example, if you asked a person to define a female standard of physical perfection in 19th century America, the person would likely describe someone Rubenesque (plump, or having a physique associated with Flemish painter Peter Paul Rubens' portraits of women). In the 21st century, however, the preference seems to be for women on the slimmer end of the spectrum. So the 19th century ideal was relative to that period, but by today's standards, that is not generally the case. But even still, there are millions of men and women whose idea of a "perfect" body is closer to that of a Sumo wrestler than it is to Lolo Jones; it's subjective and relative.

In addition, because people are on a constant quest to achieve Self-Actualization—reaching and fulfilling one's maximum potential—if a person is successful at attaining all of the attributes that they or someone else has defined to determine one's perfection, the now-perfect person would eventually want something more or different than "perfection" in which he or she finds him or herself, signifying that the person is no longer perfect—meaning that **the person was never perfect in the first place!** We see this often with people who strike it rich financially. All their lives they dreamed about how much better life would be if they had $1 million dollars. But once the person obtains $1 million dollars, the person will then be dissatisfied with the "paltry" million dollars and will need even more money to fuel the satisfaction engine.

These examples illustrate that not only is perfection elusive, if at all possible, it will never truly satisfy a person, even if it *is* somehow magically achieved, leading the "perfect" person to seek a "*new* perfection" that will never be attained. This means that the "perfection" the person once attained was not really "perfection" after all.

The Elusiveness of Perfection

Acknowledgment that you are not perfect afterall

Acknowledgment that you are not perfect

① I am not Perfect

I seek a "new perfection"

④

② I attain perfection

Belief that you have achieved perfection

I am still not satisfied

③

Desire for a more perfect perfection

Keeping Up With the Joneses

The example I previously referenced, about the person wishing for $1 million, is an example of a person not seeking "total perfection" wherein every aspect of their lives is perfect, but "perfection" and fulfillment in some aspect(s) of their lives. For example, some people define their perfection as having a single attribute fulfilled, like being financially "rich" or professionally "successful." Some theorize that this desire to be "rich" or "successful" is not simply a means to provide the nouveau riche or over-achiever with a comfortable life, but is, instead, relative to some standard of well-being (financial wealth or career success, for instance) defined by others.

In his 1965 book *Deceit, Desire, and the Novel: Self and Other in Literary Structure*, author and former Stanford University Professor Rene Girard defined the term *mimesis* or what has come to be called the "mimetic theory of desire," as an unconscious form of imitation that invariably leads to competition. He wrote of the people whom we seek to imitate that we "depict them not as they are but as they should be:" perfect.

> "… when a painter wants to become famous for his art he tries to imitate the originals of the best artists he knows; the same rule applies to most important jobs or exercises … In the same way, Amadis was the pole, the star, the sun for brave and amorous knights, and we others who fight under the banner of love

and chivalry should imitate him. …whomever imitates him best will come closest to perfect chivalry."

Mimesis is a form of subliminal imitation in which people desire things simply because they are desired by someone else. According to Mel Schwartz, a psychotherapist and the author of *The Art of Intimacy, The Pleasure of Passion*, perfectionists tend to think that other people are somehow better or superior to them, so they need to be without flaw just to catch up. Schwartz's assertion is similar to what is more commonly known as the phenomenon of "Keeping up with the Joneses."

The phrase "Keeping up with the Joneses" was popularized when a comic strip of the same name was created by cartoonist Arthur R. "Pop" Momand. It debuted in April 1913 in the *New York Globe*, the *World-Herald* (Omaha, Nebraska) and other newspapers. According to the *New York Times*:

> Mr. Momand said the strip was based on his observations of life in Cedarhurst, N.Y., where he and his wife had lived ''far beyond their means'' in a vain effort to keep pace with ''the well-to-do class." The Joneses were often mentioned in the strip, but never seen. The cartoonist said he considered using the name Smith, but decided on Jones because it was more ''euphonious."

Most commonly, "Keeping up with the Joneses" refers to a person using his or her neighbor as a benchmark for social class or the accumulation of material goods. To fail to "keep up with the Joneses" is perceived as demonstrating socio-economic or cultural inferiority. Disappointingly, the Joneses are only perfect until we achieve what they have and become what they are.

Mimetic desires—the desire to have what our neighbors have—are aroused not by the object itself, but by our *desire* for the object. Inevitably, competition becomes its own end, and the object of our desire becomes irrelevant as our previously cordial neighbors become rivals. An example is when two children play with toys: one child grabs a toy and starts to play with it. When it is observed by the other child, she wants to play with that same toy; not because the child necessarily wants the toy, but because the child wants what the other child is playing with. Eventually, what was once a fun play-date dissolves into two children fighting and crying, leaving both unfulfilled. This idea of mimetic desires relates to the story of the person who gained that desired $1 million believing that the money would put him in the same league as his affluent neighbors (on whom, incidentally, the envious person ascribed perfection). The envious person would realize that having money didn't help him achieve Joneses-like perfection or fulfillment, because—according to Girard—his desire to keep up with the Joneses was driven by just that, his *desire* for what they *have*, instead of the desire to be comfortable and satisfied, as he initially believed the neighbors to be. Eventually, the person would seek a "new perfection" and accept that even when he had the $1 million he was neither perfect nor like his neighbors.

A More Perfect Perfection = Imperfection

The elusiveness of perfection, mimetic desires, and keeping up with the Joneses all combine to provide useful instruction that **perfection is unattainable and unachievable**. As these postulates reveal, if a person is ever able to actually articulate perfection and somehow attain it, the person's mimetic desires, changing paradigm of life, and/or the person's need for Self-Actualization will create a desire in the person to want something more or something different—a "more perfect" perfection. And if a person believes that there is more that he or she could obtain, achieve, or become—beyond the person's existing state of "perfection"—then the person cannot actually be perfect or have achieved a state of perfection since perfection suggests a state of flawlessness, a condition whereby your action or performance attains a level of excellence that cannot be exceeded. To want more than you have, the desire to achieve more than you have achieved, or the desire to become more than you currently are reveal that you could somehow still be "better" than you are, and a desire to be "better" implies that you have not achieved the elusive state of perfection. This desire to be "better" is consistent with Maslow's theoretical Self-Actualization need, which argues that people want to be the best that we can become; we want to be our best selves possible, even if our best self is short of any definition of perfection.

Self-Actualization is about the desire and pursuit to be our best possible selves and not about peaking at some definition of "perfection," to the point where there is nothing more a person can improve. If we ever do max-out our Self-Actualization and achieve a state where: we have no further desires or needs; where we have done and learned all there is to do and learn; where we have perfect, loving relationships; where we have achieved our physical ideal; where we feel no pain; where we have no fears; where we feel no envy; where we are never sad; where we are always happy; where we don't make mistakes; where we have raised perfect children who all received 4-year full academic scholarships to Yale, Harvard, Stanford, MIT, and Wharton; and where we never experience the physical and mental impact of aging, then we haven't achieved perfection; we have most assuredly *died*.

Perfection is like complete satisfaction: we spend our lives pursuing it, while subconsciously knowing that we will never achieve or attain it. In 1959, during his first team meeting as the coach of the Green Bay Packers, legendary championship-winning coach Vince Lombardi (after whom the National Football League's Super Bowl championship trophy is named) instructed: "Gentlemen, we will chase perfection, and we will chase it relentlessly, knowing all the while we can never attain it. But, along the way, we shall catch excellence."

So, is it worthwhile to seek perfection, to pursue it, or is the pursuit of perfection irrational?

3

The Quest *for* Perfection

As I proposed in the previous chapter, perfection is nei-ther attainable nor achievable. So, if "perfection" is not attainable, then is it worth pursuing? What are the potential benefits and risks associated with the pursuit of perfection? The idea that a person's pursuit of perfection could have negative consequences introduces the topic of *perfectionism*.

Perfectionism is the *need* for a person to be or appear to be perfect, flawless. There is a difference between a person's *desire* to be perfect and their pursuit thereof, and a person's inherent *need* for perfection. If a person wants to be perfect, that person has identified a flaw or something unsatisfactory that he or she would like to eliminate, believing that the elimination of the flaw would make the person … well … *flawless*, perfect. If a person has an inherent need to be or to be perceived as perfect—just as humans have an inherent need for food and water for survival—then such a person's pursuit of perfection could be considered a disorder. As Ash-er R. Pacht wrote in *American Psychologist*:

> I would say that any person who thinks he or she is perfect almost certainly has real psycho-logical problems, and the same is probably true of any person who wants to be perfect.

In a 1978 article published in *Psychology: A Journal of Human Behavior*, psychologist Don Hamachek argued that perfectionists can be categorized as either "normal perfec-tionists" or "neurotic perfectionists." According to Ham-achek, normal perfectionists set realistic standards for themselves, derive pleasure from their hard work, and are capable of choosing to be less precise in certain situations. Neurotic perfectionists, on the other hand, place usually unattainable demands and levels of performance on themselves, believe that everything they do is unsatisfactory, and are unable to relax their unattainably-high standards.

Psychologists claim that distinguishing between these two types of perfectionists would help reveal the individuals who would likely end up facing negative consequences, in the long run, from their unattainably-high standards. Neurotic perfectionists, for example, feel a constant need to achieve perfection and become frustrated by their inability to do so, which leads to excessive self-criticism. This is to be expected. Since the neurotic perfectionist leaves no room for errors, then no matter what activities they engage in toward achieving their perfection-goal, the end result will almost always be failure and disappointment. The failure to achieve the unrealistic perfection-goals they set for themselves puts them at risk for disorders, such as: depression, alcoholism, coronary heart disease, anorexia, and at its worst, suicide.

Normal perfectionists (also called "adaptive" and "personal standards perfectionists") are often high achievers, drivers, and go-getters. For the normal perfectionist, the pursuit of perfection is healthier because they set *realistic*, attainable standards for themselves, and they don't dwell on their failure to achieve the lofty goals they set, at least not to the point that they become neurotic. Normal perfectionists set high personal standards and, though achieving or attaining perfection is not possible, they understand that striving for it can lead to improvement and positive results. For example, a concert pianist who relentlessly practices to play Charles-Valentin Alkan's "Concerto for Solo Piano," Opus number 39/8-10 (arguably the most difficult piano piece ever written) *perfectly* might never achieve perfection, but her pursuit of perfection will undoubtedly help her to improve her performance of not only "Concerto for Solo Piano," but also other musical pieces.

Normal perfectionism is also a good trait for those who want to excel at their job, craft, or profession because—as with the concert pianist—the pursuit is what helps you improve your vocation. Most professional athletes are also normal perfectionists (rather than neurotic perfectionists), because they *strive for perfection*. And when an athlete, for instance, an NFL quarterback doesn't complete 100% of his thrown passes—but, instead, completes only 65% of his passes, which is enough for his team to win—the quarterback might be disappointed that some of his throws were off-target and not caught, but he puts the less-than-perfect performance behind him and prepares to be perfect in the next game.

Some say that any perfectionist trait is damaging, including normal or "healthy" perfectionism, which they argue is a misnomer and an oxymoron. Paul Hewitt, a practicing psychologist and professor at the University of British Columbia, does not agree that perfectionism can sometimes serve as a healthy motivation for achieving one's goals. "I don't think needing to be perfect is in any way adaptive," he says. Those who disagree with Hewitt would probably respond by saying that Hamachek's use of "normal perfectionism" is an expression of the opposite of "neurotic perfectionism" (akin to other terms, including: "socially prescribed perfectionism," "self-oriented perfectionism," and "other-oriented perfectionism") and is intended to illustrate the degrees of perfectionism. I believe that normal perfectionism ("healthy striving," as some have termed it) is the pursuit of excellence more so than it is truly the pursuit of the unattainable.

The University of Texas at Austin's Counseling and Mental Health Center issued a report that does a very nice-yet-simple job of pointing out the differences between neurotic perfectionism ("Perfectionism") and normal perfectionism ("Healthy Striving"), which I have re-created in the table below.

Perfectionism	Healthy Striving
Setting standards beyond reach and reason	Setting standards that are high but within reach
Never being satisfied by anything less than perfection	Enjoying the process as well as the outcome
Becoming depressed when faced with failure or disappointment	Bouncing back quickly from failure or disappointment
Being preoccupied with fears of failure and disapproval	Keeping normal anxiety and fear of failure within bounds
Seeing mistakes as evidence of unworthiness	Seeing mistakes as opportunities for growth and learning
Becoming overly defensive when criticized	Reacting positively to constructive criticism

Neurotic perfectionism and self-criticism are generally associated with dissatisfaction with certain aspects of oneself. It becomes a statement that "I cannot accept myself as I am today; I'm not good enough just as I am." This is the underlying driver for people's desire to be perfect or achieve perfection. Before we can get off the destructive path of self-dissatisfaction and onto the path toward fulfillment, we must first silence the overly-critical inner-voices and accept and embrace who we are.

Self-Acceptance

> "Because one believes in oneself, one doesn't try to convince others. Because one is content with oneself, one doesn't need others' approval. Because one accepts oneself, the whole world accepts him or her."
>
> — *Lao Tzu,* philosopher

The first step on the road to being the best-you-possible begins with the acknowledgment that **you are not perfect**, that "something" in your current state of being is unsatisfactory and does not meet your expectations or aspirations. To do this, you must embrace who you are—warts and all—and truly accept the fact that you are who you are, you are how you are, and you are what you are, all with the understanding that you will never be perfect, but you can be better if you truly want to be. Sure, we might want things to be different tomorrow or in the future, but, in the present, we must accept things as they are. To do otherwise is certain to lead to a life of misery and discontentment. Far too often, we misguidedly believe that our imperfections are roadblocks to our fulfillment, happiness, and peace of mind. Embracing oneself and accepting that the imperfections we carry are natural—because no one is or can be perfect—and not "our fault," we can begin the process of achieving our realistic aspirations with the knowledge that, while we might not achieve perfection, we can become happier with ourselves and more fulfilled. Self-acceptance is about simply liking ourselves more, if not necessarily loving ourselves.

Once we acknowledge that "something" in our current state of being is unsatisfactory and not meeting our expectations or aspirations, we must then specifically identify that which we believe to be unsatisfactory about ourselves, our condition, or our station. When we do, we not only heighten our self-awareness toward things that hold us back from being more fulfilled, but we can also begin to work our way above the feelings of shame, guilt, underachievement, or embarrassment that we may hold onto because something in our lives or something about ourselves falls short of what we would like them to be. As we work our way above the feelings of shame, guilt, underachievement, and embarrassment, we stop beating ourselves up for our imperfections and our self-esteem (feeling of self-worth) improves, because we genuinely begin to feel better about ourselves. I believe there is an association between self-acceptance and self-esteem—which is necessary to achieve Self-Actualization; self-esteem is a function of self-acceptance and vice-versa. Leon Seltzer, a clinical psychologist and the author of *Paradoxical Strategies in Psychotherapy* posits that the two are not the same, as some people believe them to be.

> Though related, self-acceptance is not the same as self-esteem. Whereas self-esteem refers specifically to how valuable, or worthwhile, we see ourselves, self-acceptance alludes to a far more global affirmation of self. When we're self-accepting, we're able to embrace all facets of ourselves—not just the positive, more "esteem-able" parts. As such, self-acceptance is unconditional, free of any qualification. We can recognize our weaknesses, limitations, and foibles, but this awareness in no way interferes with our ability to fully accept ourselves.

Self-esteem—whether high or low—is about self-worth. It is the *value* we ascribe to ourselves, how we perceive our value to the world, and how valuable we think we are to others. People with low self-esteem, for example, are more distressed by failure, blame others for their shortcomings, and tend to interpret non critical comments as critical. On the other hand, People with high self-esteem have an ability to make mistakes and learn from them; they don't place blame at the feet of others and they use failure as an opportunity for growth and development. The individual with high self-esteem has the ability to accept his or her shortcomings, which is a form of self-acceptance; understanding one's personal strengths and limitations, acknowledging one's imperfections, and having the confidence that one can make improvements in his or her life.

Self-acceptance is about liking and even loving ourselves more, the operative word being *ourselves*. Far too often, people with the neurotic perfectionism trait and even people who merely want to be "perfect" ("I want to look like Raquel Welch") somehow feel as though their present imperfect selves makes them less worthy or less significant in the eyes of other people. Because of these feelings of inadequacy, these people engage in approval-seeking behaviors, which often manifest themselves as trying to live up to someone else's standards. This type of behavior, it has been argued, dates back to one's childhood where the child seeks out praise from its parents or caretakers as a sign of "goodness." Some people carry that approval-seeking behavior with them into adulthood, while others realize that they are no longer kids and that they must define themselves for themselves, if they are to be happy on their own terms. To quote the self-proclaimed "black-lesbian feminist mother lover poet" Audre Lorde: "If I didn't define myself for myself, I would be crunched into other people's fantasies for me and eaten alive."

Complacency and self-acceptance

The discussion of self-acceptance begs the question: once a person accepts him or herself and embraces the person they are—warts and all—will they still be motivated to become better or to strive to excel at some endeavor?

My position is that self-acceptance is not the end, but rather the on-ramp to becoming a better you. For example, if Sam, the college student who consistently achieved a grade-point-average (G.P.A.) of 2.5 (which correlates to slightly better than a "C" average), stopped beating himself up because he was not living up to his parents' academic performance standards, and accepted the fact that he is not Albert Einstein, but is instead, Sam, the average student, he would undoubtedly start to feel better about himself. And the better he felt about himself, the more his self-esteem would increase, leading him to believe that he could achieve more. So while Sam accepts that he might never be a 4.0 ("A") student, it does not mean that he would not want to pursue "A" grades in his future courses, understanding that though he may fall short of straight-As ("normal perfectionism"), his best self might be better than the "C"-student he currently is; he might actually be a "B"-student or better.

Maslow's theory of human motivation suggests that Sam would be intrinsically motivated to earn better grades to satisfy his Esteem need (self-respect, the respect of others, and success) and even a Love need (the acceptance of his parents—which, incidentally, Maslow argues is a prerequisite to achieving the Esteem need).

The road to contentment

In the end, the only perfection that matters is "your perfection," and the only aspirations that matter for you are your own aspirations, however you define them, based on your ambitions and potential. "Your Perfection" is being the best "you" that you can be. It is about accomplishing the most you can with what you have. It is about charting your own course for happiness and fulfillment. It is about Self-Actualization. Though "your perfection" might not meet the standard that someone else or society, in general, has determined defines perfection, it is nonetheless *your* perfection.

When we are at peace with the reality of who we are and what we can realistically become or achieve, then—as long as we have accomplished what we could feasibly have become or achieved—we put ourselves on the path toward attaining that which we sought by seeking perfection in the first place: contentment and fulfillment.

4

Stages of Improvement

THE THREE STAGES OF IMPROVEMENT

As people embark on a mission toward improving them-selves, their performance, or their circumstances, the change and improvement they experience is gradual; one cannot go from dud-to-stud in one fell swoop. As with Abra-ham Maslow's hierarchy of needs, whereby a person must satisfy his lower-level basic physiological needs for food and shelter before he or she can be concerned with finding love or companionship, so, too, must a person move from her current state to some intermediate improvement stages before achieving optimization. Based on my experience of helping people improve from some initial, undesired state to becoming the best that they could feasibly become, people progress gradually through **Three Stages of Improvement**:

Stage 1: Dissatisfaction. A person in the Dissatisfaction Stage finds him/herself in an undesired state, resulting in unhappiness, disappointment, and/or non-fulfillment;

Stage 2: Enlightenment. A person progresses into the En-lightenment Stage when s/he accepts her/his current cir-cumstance as a part of life, understands the reason(s) for her/his dissatisfaction, and envisions and believes there is a way forward toward measurable, significant improvement;

Stage 3: Optimization. After a person has progressed from her/his state of dissatisfaction and has become enlightened through self-acceptance and hope, s/he then defines a path forward which s/he follows toward being better than s/he is today. As s/he follows the path, s/he begins to make gradual improvements in her/his life toward becoming the best person that s/he can be and performing at the highest level at which s/he is capable; this highest level of capability is the Optimization Stage.

Three Stages of Improvement

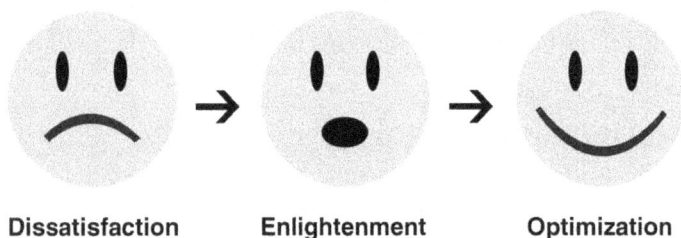

| Dissatisfaction | Enlightenment | Optimization |

For example, a form of disfluent speech is *stuttering*—a speech disorder in which sounds, syllables, or words are repeated or prolonged, disrupting a person's normal speech flow. Roughly three million Americans are affected by the disorder. A Public Opinion Survey of Human Attributes was conducted querying more than 1,200 adult respondents in 11 countries about their opinions of people who stutter. The data from the studies analyzed show that people around the world perceive stuttering almost as negatively as mental illness and obesity, and more negatively than wheelchair use. In addition, the data show an unsubstantiated stereotype that people who stutter are nervous, shy, and fearful. Such misperceptions and stereotypes become self-fulfilling prophecies in many cases, because people who stutter actually become nervous about speaking publicly in groups and fearful of the opinions people might form should they stutter and not speak fluently. This can be especially difficult for prepubescent teens who also have to cope with the natural awkwardness that young people experience during that growth and development stage.

Actress Emily Blunt (whose movie credits include: *The Devil Wears Prada*, *The Adjustment Bureau*, *Looper*, and *Edge of Tomorrow*) was a stutterer in her early teens. In an interview with *Vulture* (a *New York* magazine entertainment site), she recounts how being asked to read a poem in class was "terrifying." When asked how she overcame her stutter, she said that she first had to gain confidence, and one of her teachers helped her develop that confidence, as well as improve her speech, eventually helping her overcome her stuttering. The teacher suggested that Emily be in the class play which, of course, she had no interest in, because she couldn't talk. The teacher then suggested, "Well, why don't you try it in a different voice? Try to do a funny voice or an accent. Maybe that would help," and it did; she was actually able to speak fluently that way. She went on to say that being able to hear herself speak fluently, albeit in a funny voice, gave her confidence to think that she could speak fluently again and again. After the night of the school play, it all became a bit easier for her until, eventually, she began to speak without a stutter, becoming able to speak as best she possibly could.

This example illustrates how Emily Blunt's speech improvement followed my sequential Three Stages of Improvement, as I described above. She did not go directly from one day being dissatisfied with her stuttering to speaking fluently the next. It was a gradual process that required her to progress from being dissatisfied with her way of speaking, to realizing that fluent speech was possible and how it was possible, to being a better speaker and, ultimately, optimizing her oratory abilities and becoming a Golden Globe Award-winning actress.

Emily Blunt's Three Stages of Improvement: Stuttering		
Dissatisfaction	**Enlightenment**	**Optimization**
Emily Blunt was a stutterer, which often embarrassed and even "terrified" her when she had to speak in front of her class.	Following her teacher's suggestion to speak in a different, funny voice, Emily realized that she *could* speak fluently, albeit in a different voice. This gave her hope that, over time, it would be possible to speak without a stutter.	After repeated performances in the school play where she spoke (fluently) in the funny voice, it became easier for her to speak fluently in her normal voice, until she was eventually able to speak fluently and completely lose her stutter.

Difference-Reduction

The process of improving from one's current Dissatisfaction Stage to the desired Optimization Stage is, in one sense, a matter of *difference-reduction*. The idea behind difference-reduction as a problem-solving concept is that there are lots of differences between a person's current unfulfilled state and the person's desired goal state. Say, for example, that Ken, an 18-year-old high school graduate who works as a used car salesman, wants to become a stockbroker. He is miserable in his current job and the thought of going into work every day makes Ken physically ill. He doesn't make very much money, so his options for entertainment and material possessions are limited. He's wanted to become a stockbroker ever since he saw the 2013 Leonardo DiCaprio film *The Wolf of Wall Street*. Ken believed that becoming a broker would provide him with financial security and prestige, two things that he imagined would bring happiness and professional fulfillment.

One day, Ken called a friend who was working on Wall Street as a stockbroker and asked his friend about the requirements for an 18-year-old used car salesman like him to become a broker. The friend rattled off the following list of requirements:

- Get a college degree, preferably an MBA degree from a "top" college;
- Take two mandatory exams (Series 7 and Series 63);
- Register with the Financial Industry Regulatory Authority ("FINRA");
- Secure interviews with your desired firms;
- Gain on-the-job experience (possibly through internships);
- Start an investment portfolio;

- Turn 21 years old (a requirement for working at some firms).

For Ken, these seven requirements were the difference between his current state (as a miserable used car salesman) and his desired goal-state (to become a stockbroker). For him to become a stockbroker, he would have to *reduce* and/ or eliminate the *differences* between his current state and his desired state—hence, the term "difference-reduction." For each difference that Ken eliminates, the total number of differences gets reduced until all differences have been eliminated, leaving no difference between Ken and "Ken the stockbroker." In other words, once all of the differences between the Ken today and the Ken he wants to become have been eliminated, there would be no differences between Ken's current state and his desired state—Ken = Stockbroker—and he would have accomplished his goal.

Difference Reduction

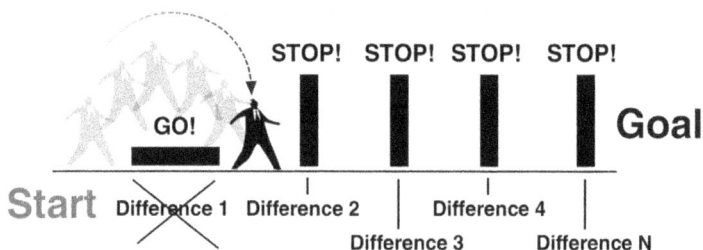

The differences between one's current state and desired state are obstacles at their worst and tasks to complete at their best. Differences are gaps that must be filled before one can achieve a goal or some desired state or condition. The difference between the size of the woman who *wants to* fit into her college blue jeans (the current state) and the size of the woman who *used to* fit into the blue jeans (the desired state) is 10 pounds. By reducing her weight by 10 pounds (the difference), the woman would become the size she was in college and able to fit into her college blue jeans. The challenge for most people who aspire to become "better" or to become their best possible selves is figuring out *how* to get from their current state to their desired state. This raises the question: What does it mean to be "better?"

What is "Better"?

Often when I work with people to help them become "better" at some pursuit, the person's goal is stated as just that: "To become 'better' than I am today." One of the first things to do when developing a plan for becoming "better" is to clearly and specifically define what one intends when expressing the desire "to be better." In an absolute sense, being "better" (used as an adjective in this context) simply means to be further or to perform at higher levels than previously. Based on this basic definition, my desire to be "better" implies that I must only "improve" over some previous standard or performance measure—regardless of the degree of improvement. For example, if I was a competitive weekend-warrior runner who competed in races and I wanted to perform "better" in the weekly 1-mile race than I did in the previous weekend's race, I would only have to look at my time from that race and improve by one second to be "better." So, if I finished last weekend's race in 10 minutes and 12 seconds, and I finished this weekend's race in 10 minutes and 11 seconds I would technically have performed better than last week, so should I be thrilled with that "accomplishment?" After all, I did accomplish my goal of performing better than I did last week, even if it was only by 1 second.

This example illustrates one of the problems with simply defining a goal as an adjective, such as the desire to be "better," or the desire to be "beautiful," or the desire to be "perfect," or even the desire to be "smarter;" and that problem is the difficulty of defining exactly what it means to be better, or beautiful, or perfect, or smarter. There is an old saying that if you can't define something you can't measure it, and if you can't measure something you can't improve it. By defining a goal simply as "to be better," if one cannot measure what being "better" means (based solely on the stated goal), then one cannot develop a plan to meaningfully improve one's goodness to know whether the vaguely-defined goal "to be better" has been meaningfully accomplished.

My definition of being "better," however, means that any *improvement* or positive changes in circumstance must be materially meaningful or impactful—it must create a behavioral change in the current state toward that which one desires to achieve or accomplish. In that sense, "being better" is relative and is within the purview of the person looking to be better. If my goal as a runner is "to win a medal by finishing in the top 3," then improving my completion time by 1 second won't help. But, if I knew that the third place winner in last week's race completed the race 1 minute and 30 seconds faster than I did, I would know the degree of improvement (of "being better") necessary for me to have a shot at third place. This redefinition of my goal is clearly defined and easily understood; it is also measurable, which means that I can develop a plan to achieve it.

Similar to "being better" is the goal to be "the best 'you' possible." What does it mean to be "the best 'you' possible?" Being the best that you can be is the point at which the potential or reality of further improvement or betterment becomes *practically* unachievable versus possibly achievable. By "practically unachievable," I mean that, though *possible*, a pursuit has reached the point where an increase in the additional effort and resources necessary to pursue greater heights or a higher level of achievement or accomplishment will not yield a corresponding increase in improvement, meaning that the extra effort you spend pursing additional gains is not worth the expected reward. This is illustrated in the diagram below.

Resource - Reward

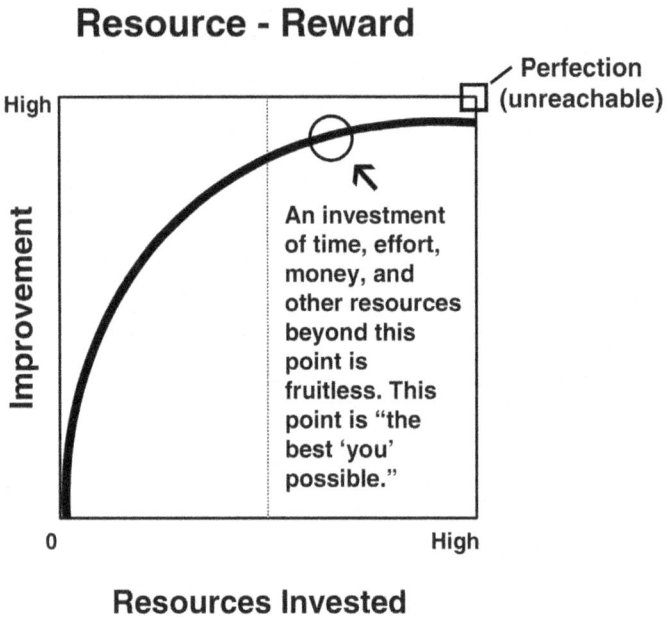

Resources Invested

The point of this diagram (which shows the relationship between resources and improvement gains) is that at some point the rational person will have to acknowledge that "perfection" is not attainable. The person will then determine the point when any additional investment is fruitless, that he or she has made all of the improvement that is practically achievable and, at that point, realize that he or she has achieved all that he or she can achieve; that they have become their "best selves possible."

5

A Model *for* Improvement

I have worked in the business world for more than 25 years in various roles, ranging from a door-to-door salesman for a now-defunct encyclopedia brand to a master-level consultant at one of the world's largest corporations. Most of these years have been spent working with under-performing organizations to help them upgrade their performance and help business professionals perform better. Through these experiences, I noticed a common thread. Whether the task was to help a company's business unit increase product sales; to help a sales professional become a better public speaker and presenter; to help an entrepreneur start a new business; or to help a public servant become more productive (so that she could spend more time with her family and less time burning the midnight oil), I found that each and every experience involved several "somethings" which, collectively, form the basis for what I call my *Model for Improvement*.

A "model" is a structure that represents a logical process for making improvements. "Improvement" comes from learning; it is about making changes that will lead to a better place. While all improvement requires change, not all change will result in improvement. A Model for Improvement is a logical process for identifying the changes to be made and the direction one must take that will lead to a higher degree of fulfillment. It is a model for *being better* and becoming the best "you" possible.

Practical Reasoning

As we begin the process of making improvements in our lives, becoming better personally or at some pursuit, getting on the path to happiness and fulfillment, or doing the best that we can with what we've got, the first question we must ask ourselves is: **Why do I want to do "it?"** Why do I want to fit into my college blue jeans? Why do I want to become a vegan? Why do I want to look like someone famous? Why do I want to be beautiful? Why do I want to weigh 105 pounds? Why do I want to master my profession? Why do I want to be better? Why do I want to be *perfect*? As you begin the process of finding answers to these questions, you will find that there is a practical *reason(s)* why you desire these things. On a theoretical or psychological level—such as Maslow's need for Self-Actualization, for instance—there are reasons why we aspire to greater things. But, critics of Maslow say it is difficult, if not impossible, to quantitatively test his self-actualization theory, which makes it difficult to test scientifically or to know when one has achieved it. The reason(s) for our aspirations must be practical. We must uncover the reason why we aspire to things on a practical level so that we will know how to go about achieving them and whether or not we have achieved them. Otherwise, we will find ourselves chasing the invisible: trying to achieve something though we don't know what it is we are trying to achieve, guaranteeing our own misery.

We can say that the reason why some people want to be beautiful, for example, is because—as quoted in the 2013

documentary *Chasing Beauty*—"Beautiful people achieve a
higher quality of life." But, the desire "to achieve a higher
quality of life" is still impractical; it's obscure and hard to
perceive. What exactly is "a higher quality of life?" Is it better health? Is it more money? Is it a better job? Is it a more
caring spouse? Is it well-adjusted children? Is it more education? The reality is that "a higher quality of life" encompasses all of the above and more, which makes achieving
it unlikely. However, if, for you, "a higher quality of life"
simply means to get out of bed each day without feeling de-
bilitating pain in your lower back, then what you really desire—from a practical standpoint—is *a pain-free lower back*.
I say "from a practical standpoint," because you can clearly
identify specific things that you can do to alleviate lower
back pain (such as: exercise, medication, physical therapy,
surgery, sleeping with a pillow between your legs, and nerve
stimulation, to name a few), and when you do these things
you can measure their effectiveness and adjust the remedies
as needed (if you find the treatments have been ineffective).
Most importantly, you will know whether or not you are
successful at achieving your goal of alleviating the back pain
because, if successful, the pain will be gone or reduced to a
manageable level.

It is important to understand that establishing ambiguous and/or unattainable goals, such as "to become a genius"
or "to be perfect," will inevitably lead to misery and disappointment, because we will either never achieve the goal or
never know whether we have achieved it or not; and if we

don't know whether or not we have achieved a goal, then chances are we have not. When we aspire to a goal, the goal must be practical and realistic so that we can not only define a path toward its achievement, but also know whether or not we have achieved it. A simple rule of thumb for knowing whether or not the goal to which you aspire is practically-defined is to ask the following question: Why do I want to achieve that goal? If the answer is not obvious, then that is a sign that the goal requires further refinement and definition. However, the reason(s) that you articulate for why you want to achieve the goal will often define the actual goal that you aspire to.

For example, if you aspire "to alleviate my back pain," the reason you want to do this is obvious. However, if you aspire "to be handsome," the reason why is not obvious, so whatever the reason (such as, "I want to find a partner"), that reason will become the real goal or, at a minimum, it will get you closer to defining what you really want to achieve by being "handsome."

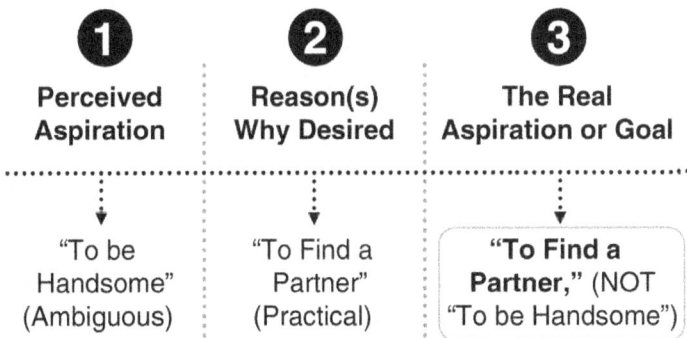

1	**2**	**3**
Perceived Aspiration	**Reason(s) Why Desired**	**The Real Aspiration or Goal**
↓	↓	↓
"To be Handsome" (Ambiguous)	"To Find a Partner" (Practical)	**"To Find a Partner,"** (NOT "To be Handsome")

This example illustrates a critical aspect of making improvements in our lives or becoming better: Whatever our aspirations, desires, or goals, we must search to find the reason(s) why we have the aspirations or desire the goals to give ourselves the best chance at attaining or achieving them, thereby increasing our chances at happiness and fulfillment (rather than misery and disappointment). This is one of the key requirements of the Model for Improvement.

CASE STUDY

Uncovering the "Real" Goal and Aspiration

Kristen is an Ambulatory Care Nurse who works for a metropolitan hospital in Washington. One afternoon while Kristen and I were discussing her situation over coffee, she told me that she was really bummed out, because she didn't make enough money to afford the luxuries or even the necessities that she hoped having such a good job would provide her. As the discussion went on, she asked me if I could work with her to develop a plan for how to increase her income within a year.

Over the months prior to our coffee meeting, Kristen had applied for several higher-paying jobs within her own hospital and at other hospitals and agencies, with no luck. While Kristen really loves her job, she was not opposed to leaving the hospital if it meant an opportunity to make more money.

My experience working with organizations and people on finance-related matters taught me that no one wants more money just for the sake of having more money; people want more money for specific reasons. Businesses typically want more money to strengthen their profit margins and increase their spendable income. Other organizations want more money to hire additional staff or engage in philanthropy. People most often want more money to pay bills and expenses or to make purchases, all to make life a little more pleasant.

So, after listening to Kristen's frustration about her financial situation, I asked her a simple question: "Why do you want to earn more money?" Without hesitation, Kristen told me that the reason she needed more money was so that she could buy a car. Apparently, Kristen's current car was older and had become unreliable. My next question to Kristen was "How much additional money do you need to buy a car?" Kristen replied that she had found a nice used car for $7,000. So, my challenge in working with Kristen was not necessarily to help her find a higher-paying job, but to help her do what she really wanted to do: to achieve her real goal of buying a car.

My approach to working with Kristen was to figure out a way for her to purchase a car with her existing salary, savings, and credit score. There are two ways to increase your disposable income: earn more money or reduce your costs and expenses. Since Kristen had already tried the former approach, we decided to focus on the latter and identify areas where Kristen could tighten her belt and reduce her expenses. Kristen had "expensive taste," so it was easy for me to execute our cost-cutting: the weekly mani-pedi became bi-weekly; authentic Japanese Kobe beef became Angus Pride; French wine became domestic; the premium cable TV package became the standard package; unlimited cell phone service became Cricket Wireless; and we placed a moratorium on new handbag purchases.

In addition, Kristen's unusual work schedule—where she worked 12-hour days on Saturdays and Sundays which equated to a full work week—allowed her to work a second job two days per week. Through spending-austerity and the second job, Kristen was able to save more than $8,000 within 9 months; money she used to purchase a more reliable car.

This engagement supported my contention that before one can work toward accomplishing a goal or even solving a problem, it is first necessary to understand one's true desires and needs. In Kristen's case, she didn't really want more money or a new job; she wanted a car; the money was just a symptom. Once I uncovered her true aspiration, I was able to work with her to achieve it.

UNDERSTANDING THE MODEL FOR IMPROVEMENT:
A PROCESS FOR ACHIEVING ONE'S GOALS
TOWARD BECOMING BETTER AND MORE FULFILLED

The work that I have done over the years toward upgrading organizational performance and helping people become better at their various pursuits has provided me with valuable insight into those things that, when developed and executed, have consistently proven to lead to positive outcomes. Over time, I have taken these demonstrated *elements of improvement* and developed them into a model—the Model for Improvement—which has successfully guided people to higher levels of performance, greater accomplishment, greater appreciation for themselves, and an overall more fulfilling existence.

"Improvement" is about bringing a person from some initial undesirable state into a more desirable or fulfilling condition. Improvement is incremental, meaning that one cannot simply go from being Forrest Gump on day-1 to Albert Einstein on day-2; it is a gradual process, as was the case when Domino's Pizza changed its core recipe to make an improved, better pizza.

In 2009, Domino's Pizza tied for last place (with Chuck-E-Cheese's) in a national pizza test-taste. The ingredients were low quality and were either frozen, canned, or premade, resulting in a bland-tasting product. While the use of these ingredients allowed Domino's to be an extremely fast pizza delivery company, when the pizzas arrived at their destinations, patrons were unimpressed. This resulted in many patrons switching brands from Domino's to better-tasting pizzas, prompting Domino's to re-vamp its entire recipe.

"This is not a slight tweak. We changed everything on our pizza from the crust up," Domino's USA President J. Patrick Doyle told *AnnArbor.com*. "We changed the crust, we changed the sauce, we changed the cheese." Domino's tested many cheeses, sauces, and crust-seasoning blends over a two-year period to develop a better pizza. With each ingredient combination, Domino's noticed a gradual improvement in the freshness, quality, and taste of its product until, eventually, they arrived at what consumers agreed was a better-tasting, much improved product. The pizza's improved taste was validated when Domino's submitted their pizzas to an independent, blind taste-test of approximately 1,800 random pizza consumers across multiple U.S. markets. In the end, Domino's Pizza beat its major competitors (Papa John's and Pizza Hut) by a wide margin.

Making improvements is a gradual process involving defining what needs to be accomplished to be "better," those things that must be changed for a person to become "better," validating that such changes will lead to improvement, and making the necessary changes. Making improvements toward becoming better is about reducing the differences between where you are today and where you want to be tomorrow. It's about Domino's Pizza reducing the differences between its bland-tasting pizza and a fresh, good-tasting pizza; a gradual process. It's about a young Jack LaLanne reducing the differences between the confidence-level of his

97-pound-weakling self and his 190-pound strong, confident ideal; a gradual process.

My Model for Improvement consists of five sequential elements that contribute to the person attaining the desired state and, ultimately, happiness and fulfillment. The five elements are:

1. Acknowledgment;

2. Identification;

3. A Genuine Desire to Change;

4. A Plan;

5. Adjustments.

Acknowledgment

Before any meaningful improvement can be made in a person's condition, station, or performance, there must be an acknowledgment (an admission, recognition, and acceptance) that "something" in the person's current state is unsatisfactory to the *person* and/or not meeting the person's expectations or aspirations. Acknowledgment and acceptance, however, is a challenge for many people, because admitting that there is a "problem" (a matter involving doubt, uncertainty, or difficulty), a stressful situation, or an unfavorable condition that exists in one's life can make people feel flawed and vulnerable. Admitting to one's self that a problem exists can threaten the person's sense of control. The person must then deal with the pain or discomfort that will likely be caused by confronting the problem, and the person may not be able to cope with the pain. So, the natural response for many people is to deny that a problem or unfavorable situation exists. By denying that a problem exists, the person is "protecting" him or herself by refusing to accept the truth about something that is happening in their lives, thereby avoiding the problem and the associated pain.

Denial—an outright refusal to admit or recognize that something has occurred or is currently occurring—is a defense mechanism; it protects a person from things that the individual cannot cope with. In some cases, initial short-term denial can be healthy, giving a person time to adjust to a painful or stressful situation. However, being in denial for any period beyond the initial short-term can prevent a person from dealing with issues that require action, such as a health crisis, for example. The first stage of coming out of denial is to acknowledge there is a problem.

To begin moving beyond denial and onto the acknowledgment path, you must ask yourself: Why change the unsatisfactory condition that befalls you? Why do you want to be "better?" What would your life be like if you could achieve your aspirations? The answers to these questions will not only help you to visualize and see as possible a better state of being, but will also serve as the foundation for defining the things to which you aspire, or your own personal **Goals**. A *goal* is the broad intended outcome of an initiative or activity in which one engages. It is something a person believes he or she must do or accomplish—as determined by the person him or herself—to become happier and more fulfilled in life. Of all the things that contribute to a person's well-being, *engagement* and *meaning* are the most crucial for leading a happy life. Goals give people a sense of purpose; they give life meaning. They provide people with hope, optimism about the future, confidence to pursue that which is possible, and the motivation to grow, develop, and better themselves and their station in life. Goals give many people a reason to live. And when a person successfully accomplishes a self-defined goal, they not only realize the benefits that accompany successful goal accomplishment (for example, being the top Los Angeles real estate agent), but they also gain the motivation to strive to become even better. In doing so, they move that much closer toward satisfying the need for Self-Actualization and becoming truly fulfilled in life.

By affording yourself the pleasure of visualizing what life as a "better you" would hold, you must not only move beyond denial, but you must also become more self-accepting. As I wrote in *Chapter 3: The Quest for Perfection*, self-acceptance is not the end, but rather the on-ramp to becoming a better you. To become more self-accepting, you must ask yourself what it is you don't accept about yourself and, as an agent of your own healing, elevate yourself from denial by understanding the reasons behind your denial. It should then become easier to define and strive to meet your *own* rational standards for self-acceptance—not society's standards.

Identification

"The most productive aspect of solving a problem is correctly identifying the real problem and its cause(s); the rest is easy."
– *Tab Edwards*

Acknowledgement and acceptance that "something" in your current state is unsatisfactory and is not meeting your expectations or aspirations is the first step toward becoming better. The next step is identifying that unsatisfactory "something" so that you can then begin to address it. The difference between Acknowledgment and Identification is like the difference between saying "I don't feel well" and saying "I don't feel well, because I have a headache." While it is good to admit that you don't feel well, you cannot get on the path toward feeling better until you identify the reason why you do not feel well—your headache. Once the headache is identified as the reason why you don't feel well, you can then treat the headache and begin to feel better.

Part of the challenge with identifying the unsatisfactory matter in our lives is ensuring that the issue we identify as the cause of our dissatisfaction or our desire to improve is in fact the "real" issue or cause, as opposed to the "perceived" issue or cause. For example, Sarah, a physically attractive woman, acknowledges that she is unfulfilled in her personal life and dissatisfied with her long-term status as a single woman. She desperately wants to meet the right person for a loving and lasting relationship. However, each time she meets someone new and goes on a few dates with the person, the person either stops calling (or e-mailing or messaging) her or becomes disinterested in continuing a relationship.

When attempting to identify the reason for a situation or "why" something happens—such as, why Sarah cannot establish a longer-term relationship—best practice is to develop a sound argument for why something has occurred or is occurring. A *sound argument* is one which is valid and the premises are all true. In other words, a sound argument has a conclusion that must be true if the premises are true—and the premises are actually *true*. The following is an example of a sound argument based on the validity of its premises:

1. All bachelors are unmarried (the major premise);
2. Bob is a bachelor (the minor premise);
3. Therefore, Bob is unmarried (the argument or conclusion).

So, if Bob is a bachelor, he must be unmarried. The truth of the conclusion (Bob is unmarried) is guaranteed by the truth of the premises; the conclusion follows logically from the premises.

However, sometimes we arrive at conclusions or make arguments based on invalid premises, leading to invalid arguments and faulty conclusions, which lead us to work toward improving or becoming better at the wrong things.

1. If it's raining and I am outdoors, my hair gets wet (major premise);

2. My hair is wet (minor premise);

3. Therefore, it's raining outside (unsound argument or conclusion).

This example of deductive reasoning is invalid, because the truth of the premises *does not* guarantee the truth of the conclusion; it is possible that my hair got wet another way besides by being out in the rain. Perhaps someone sprayed me with a water hose.

The process of arriving at a conclusion (making a sound argument) based on the validity of an argument's premises is a form of deductive reasoning whereby a valid argument can be made or a conclusion drawn from valid premises. In the case of Sarah, the perennially single physician, she could deduce—as she has done—that the reason she is single is because potential partners are intimidated by her professional accomplishments.

1. People are professionally insecure when dating physicians (major premise);

2. I am a physician (minor premise);

3. Therefore, people are insecure when dating me, because I am a physician (conclusion).

This is an invalid argument and conclusion based on faulty reasoning, because there could be other reasons why people are "insecure" about dating Sarah (if, that is even true) besides the fact that she is a physician.

By answering a series of questions about herself and her

history of failed relationships, and by applying deductive reasoning, Sarah began to build sound arguments for why she has been unable to maintain lasting relationships, ultimately uncovering the most probable reasons why. This enabled her to address the reasons in hopes of finding a longer-term partner and, hopefully, true love. Sarah asked herself and answered the following **Issue Identification Questions (IIQs)**:

Issue Identification Question #1: What are the possible reasons why people in your undesirable situation are in the situation in which you find yourself? (For example, why do people abandon new relationships or "stop calling" after a series of dates?)

As illustrated by the invalid argument above (an argument or conclusion based on faulty reasoning), there are many possible reasons why a person may find him or herself in a particular situation. The purpose of IIQ is to prompt you to create a proverbial laundry list of possible reasons to consider. This "brainstorming" process will encourage open, unbiased thinking by requiring you to consider and list any possible reason you can imagine without concern for the degree of applicability to the issue under consideration. It will help you generate ideas and creative possibilities to consider as you engage in the process of identifying the most likely causes of the issue or problem.

Applying this question to Sarah's inability to find lasting love (for example, why do people abandon new relationships or "stop calling" after a series of dates?), her brainstorm list of possible reasons includes:

- Possible Reason 1: The person perceives you to have an unflattering, prickly attitude;
- Possible Reason 2: The person thinks you are "phony" or disingenuous;
- Possible Reason 3: The person is intimidated by your professional success;
- Possible Reason 4: It is so easy to get dates (due to online dating sites) that people decided to check out other date options instead of going on a repeat date with Sarah;
- Possible Reason N: The person does not like your friends.

Applying deductive reasoning logic, Sarah might conclude that one of the reasons why she cannot maintain a lasting relationship is because her dates perceive her to have a bad attitude:

1. Some people perceive successful women who—on a first date—proudly discuss their success as being bossy and cold (major premise);

2. I am a successful woman who always discusses my professional achievements on a first date (minor premise);

3. Therefore, people perceive me as being bossy and cold (conclusion).

In this case, Sarah's conclusion is sound and could very well be valid. Dating coach Rachel Greenwald, author of the book *Why He Didn't Call You Back: 1,000 Guys Reveal What They REALLY Thought About You After Your Date*, conducted in-depth interviews with 1,000 single men, asking them why they hadn't called women back after a date. The primary reason she discovered was that, while women think their date is intimidated by her success, the date actually perceives the woman as argumentative, controlling, overly independent, and not feminine or warm.

Issue Identification Questions #2: What would a "fixed" problem look or feel like?

Earlier, I discussed "difference-reduction" as a problem-solving method whereby a person defines a state or condition to which he or she aspires and identifies the differences between him or herself today and him or herself as they would like to be. The identified differences are gaps that must be filled before one can achieve a goal or some desired state or condition. This raises an important point: **if you cannot visualize something, you cannot become it or achieve it**. This is a similar sentiment to what is commonly stated in the business world (but is also applicable in our personal lives): **if you cannot measure something, you cannot improve it**. You want to be a better parent, what does being a "better parent" look like to you? You want to be a better student, then how will you know that you have accomplished this goal? You want to be a faster reader, then how many ad-

ditional words-per-minute must your speed improve by before you are satisfied that you have become a "faster reader?"
You want to be a more confident person, then what do you
as a more "confident person" look like? If you cannot measure or define a "better parent" or a "better student" or a
"faster reader" or a more "confident person," then it will be
extremely difficult, if at all possible, to become these things.

Studies have shown a link between thoughts and behaviors. This thought-behavior link is very important for
achieving your aspirations because—just as with the benefits
of visualization in sports performance improvement—visualizing (your thoughts) gives you opportunities to "practice"
being that which you imagine or aspire to; and the more
we practice something, the closer we come to achieving our
ideal. If you imagine (visualize) the future with you already
having accomplished your goals or achieved your aspirations, you can begin to imagine that vision of yourself in as
much detail as you can conjure up: Where do you live? How
is your family? Who do you hobnob with? What emotions
are you feeling? What plans are you making? How did you
get there?! This type of visualization provides motivation to
go out and work extra hard to achieve that which you visualize.

Issue Identification Questions #3: What is the difference between you today and the "you" you want to become (the "fixed"
problem or the desired state)?

Previously, I used the difference-reduction example of Ken

the used car salesman who wanted to become a stockbroker. Ken envisioned becoming a broker, learned what it would take to become a broker—the difference between his current self and his desired state—and began accomplishing the requirements and minimizing the differences, each time moving closer to his dream: becoming a certified stockbroker. Ken's pursuit indicates that visualization must be accompanied by action. It is not enough to simply want to accomplish or achieve something; you must take action to make it happen.

Issue Identification Question #4: What did you learn from your past experiences, the similar experiences of others, and the feedback loop?

The "feedback loop" is a review process that involves soliciting feedback from those with information that can help you understand the causes of and reasons for the outcome of an event. The feedback loop also includes your own review and interpretation of events and the causes of and reasons for that outcome. In Sarah's case, this would include contacting former dates who hadn't wanted to be in a longer-term relationship with her and asking them to be forthright and tell her why. Through this process, Sarah will—hopefully—not only receive feedback on why a relationship didn't work for them, but also a list of things she can improve on and a list of things that her past dates considered turn-offs and non-starters. She might learn that her past dates thought she was high-maintenance or that they were only looking for sex or that they thought she was wonderful, but she was of a different religion or that she smokes cigarettes or that her attire was date-inappropriate.

When Sarah reflects on the dates from her own recollection, she might discover other things that, if she had it to do over again, she would change. Between the feedback from the past dates themselves and her own recollections, Sarah could compile a list of reasons to add to those generated from the brainstorming session in Issue Identification Question #1.

Issue Identification Questions #5: What do you want to change or believe you need to change? Reasons and Causes.

Using the answers from Issue Identification Questions #1 to 4, create a list of possible reasons and causes for why you are in the undesirable condition or state in which you find yourself. This list of possible reasons and causes will provide insight into the changes that need to be made for you to make your desired improvements toward becoming the best that you can become; it will help you answer the question, "What do you want or need to change?"

Without getting into a philosophical dissertation on actions, reason, and causes—for contextual simplicity—I will consider *reasons* and *causes* as follows: a "reason" can be thought of as a motivation *for* something happening; and the reason *why* that thing happened is the "cause." For instance, in the example of single Sarah, Sarah received feedback from her past dates that one "reason" why they did not pursue a relationship was because they perceived Sarah to be "bossy." The "cause" of her dates perceiving her as bossy was because Sarah talked incessantly about her very impressive professional accomplishments. The logic follows that the *cause* of the dates perceiving Sarah as bossy (a *reason* why the dates fled) was Sarah's bragging about her accomplishments; in this case, *bragging caused the reason* why dates ended.

If Sarah composed a lonely-heart list of reasons why she is unfulfilled in her personal life, the list might look like this:

Sarah's current unsatisfactory condition: personal lack of fulfillment		
Issue	**Reasons for the Issue**	**Causes**
Dissatisfaction with my long-term status as a single woman; I cannot maintain lasting relationships. (Sarah is looking to satisfy what Abraham Maslow defined as her Love Need).	Dates perceive me as bossy	Talking too much about my professional achievements on the first date before the person gets to know "me."
	Dates perceived me as high-maintenance	Talking too much about my professional achievements on the first date before the person gets to know "me."
	Dates were only looking for sex	I appropriately sent the message that I am not interested in a one-night stand.
	I was of a different religion than my dates	My religion differs from that of many of my dates.
	I smoke cigarettes. This was a major turn-off for most, if not all, of the dates.	I have a nicotine addiction.

Summarizing the list of issues uncovered through the Issue Identification Questioning activity will help you to productively progress through the improvement process by preparing you to engage in the ensuing Desire and Planning elements of the Model for Improvement.

Genuine Desire to Change

A philosopher friend of mine, Bobby Smith, says that we fear things in direct proportion to our ignorance and lack of understanding of them. With this as a premise, any activity for which we have no experience (and therefore, little understanding) is somewhat fear-inducing. When people are asked to make changes, we are often being asked to do something that we have no experience with and no knowledge of. For many, resistance to change is due to the fear of the unknown, and, according to Smith, we fear change because change and its potential outcomes are unknown to us. These unknown outcomes could bring with them discomfort at best, and physical pain, failure, or tragedy at worst. Think about it: why are you afraid to walk down dark alleys at night?

The unknown outcomes of some change could lead to painful experiences; the threat of pain induces fear in people. Fear is one of the most powerful human emotions; fear can prevent people from engaging in activities that could be in their own best interest. In addition, fear has an evolutionary benefit in that it fuels an instinct to keep safe (for example, being naturally fearful of approaching a lion). On the down side, however, fear can keep us from making the changes necessary for us to achieve our aspirations and become the best that we can become; it is one of the most significant obstacles to achieving personal success.

Fear and pain-avoidance are reasons why many people seek perfection. Perfection, they argue, means never having to change or improve, and never experiencing disappointment, sadness, personal pain, rejection, or the bad experiences that often result from change. The truth is that these unpleasant feelings and emotions are normal, and to not experience them is to be either a zombie or psychopathic. We learn from these feelings and emotions; experiencing them teaches us to not only learn to cope with them, but also how to mitigate or avoid them. To appreciate happiness, we must know what it is to be unhappy; to avoid pain, we must experience and appreciate pain. Imagine what life would be like if we could not feel pain.

Ashlyn Blocker is a 5-year-old kindergartner from Patterson, Georgia. In the school's cafeteria, Ashlyn's teachers put ice in Ashlyn's chili, because, even if the chili is scalding, she'll gulp it down anyway. Ashlyn is among the small number of people in the world with pain insensitivity, a condition known as Congenital Insensitivity to Pain with Anhidrosis, or CIPA—a rare genetic disorder that makes her unable to feel pain. "Some people would say that's a good thing. But no, it's not," says Tara Blocker, Ashlyn's mother.

Imagine not being able to feel pain. As a child, the possibility would have existed that you could have gouged out your eyeballs while exploring them as children do (because you didn't feel pain). Left unattended, you would see no fear in climbing to the top of your parents' SUV and "flying" like Superman, because you would not know the pain associated with hitting the concrete head-first—an event that could lead to death. We experience pain for a reason; pain is a teacher. It helps us to change behaviors to survive. We experience disappointment for a reason: it helps us to change the way we do things and make improvements and evolve as a species. We experience discomfort for a reason: it is our body's way of telling us that something needs to be altered or fixed for us to improve and feel better.

The common thread running through all of our undesirable feelings, thoughts, and emotions such as fear, pain, discomfort, sadness, disappointment, loneliness, rejection, and insecurity is the need for *change* to improve the situations that rouse these feelings, thoughts, and emotions. Improvement is about making changes that will lead us in a "new direction;" **all improvement requires change**. You want to make a better cake, you must change the recipe; you want to improve your physique, you must change your diet and activity level; you want to increase the amount of money you make, you must change the work you are doing today; and you want to improve your grades, you must change your study habits. Improvement requires change, and to make change possible, you must confront your negative feelings, thoughts, and emotions.

When we suppress our negative feelings, thoughts, and emotions a funny thing happens: we think about them even *more*, which raises our stress levels and strengthens negative feelings even beyond their original undesirable levels. Consider this simple example: Think of your favorite junk food, dessert, or food-based guilty pleasure; let's assume that *ice cream* is your guilty pleasure. Now, assume that you are on a diet this week and want to avoid eating ice cream, but the ice cream is sitting in your freezer waiting to be devoured. Every day you will think about that ice cream that is within arms' reach, causing you to be anxious, frustrated, and even stressed. Why? You are trying to avoid the negative consequences of eating that ice cream while you are dieting; and when we try to avoid things, we have a tendency to think about those things until the distracting object or threat is removed. Once it is removed, we can then have peace of mind. The easiest way to eliminate the frustration of having the ice cream available-yet-untouchable is to eat it (and, unfortunately experience a slight setback in your diet), give it away, or discard it. Once the distracting ice cream is gone—once you have confronted and dealt with it—you will no longer stress over it and you will be able to focus on your diet, helping you to achieve your weight-loss goal more easily.

When we try to avoid or suppress negative elements in our lives, the daily effort of trying to suppress or avoid them leads us to dwell on them, causing frustration, stress (and all health risks associated with stress), and general misery. By forcing ourselves to deal with the "ice cream"—by discarding it, for instance—the frustration and stress associated with having it in your freezer will be reduced, as the urge to eat the no-longer-readily-available ice cream dissipates.

Allowing ourselves to experience and then confront undesirable feelings, thoughts, emotions, experiences, and situations will enable us to make the changes necessary to move beyond them. By doing so, we find ourselves with fewer obstacles to overcome—increasing our chances of successfully accomplishing our goals—as we pursue our aspirations and try to reach our potential, becoming our best possible selves.

Are you willing to change?

As I wrote previously, people resist change because of the perceived risk and fear associated with the unknown. If I change my sucky job and get a new job, will the unfamiliar new job be worse than my current, known, sucky job? What If I am bad at the new job and I get fired? That's a risk. The possible negative consequences of such a change frighten me. Maybe I want to become more "spiritually enlightened" by moving from Catholicism to Buddhism, but the thought of going to the Buddha, Dharma, and Sangha for refuge is an unknown and somewhat frightening. So should I stick with the "known" (Catholicism) and live a ho-hum spiritual existence or should I risk the "unknowns" of Buddhism for a chance to become more spiritually satisfied? Will doing so consign me to "Hell"? Yikes!

Change is not easy. As humans, we are predisposed to the status quo for self-preservation. Yet, as humans, we have an unquenchable thirst for knowledge and exploration—catalysts for new discoveries and human progress. But, without change, there can be no improvement, no progress. So we must often motivate ourselves to accept change and all its associated risks, and experience the positive benefits that change brings.

For change to happen in your life you, and only you,

must be ready and willing to make the necessary changes to achieve your aspirations. To quote iconic American artist Andy Warhol: "When people are ready to, they change. They never do it before then, and sometimes, they die before they get around to it. You can't make them change if they don't want to, just like when they do want to, you can't stop them."

Just as we must be able to visualize that to which we aspire to realize it, we must also visualize the positive benefits that will befall us should we make life changes. This will motivate us to not only *desire* change, but also to make necessary changes for us to improve our lives.

To begin the process of visualizing, it is helpful to consider your answers to the following questions:

- What would your life be like if you could achieve your aspirations?
- Why would you change the unsatisfactory condition that encumbers you?
- Why do you want to be "better"?
- Are you willing to make changes in your life or are you 100% satisfied with your life as it is today?
- Other than "uncertainty," what is preventing you from making changes for improvement?
- Would you be happy and personally fulfilled if you did nothing, and kept things exactly the way they are today? If not, why not?
- Are you willing to work at becoming better even if the changes you need to make do not happen overnight?

- How will you avoid trying to change things you cannot control, and focus on changing those that you can?
- During the process of making life changes, it is important to reward yourself for small accomplishments. How will you reward yourself as you make progress?

The answers to these questions will not only help you to visualize and imagine a better state of being, but will also serve as the foundation for defining the things to which you aspire—your personal Goals.

6

A Plan (Strategy)

AND ITS IMPORTANCE IN
THE MODEL FOR IMPROVEMENT

A "Plan" is a "Strategy" and a Strategy is a Plan. Whichever term is used, they both can be considered a roadmap to get you from point-A to point-B. By definition, a strategy is a plan to achieve objectives—measurable targets that have been established to help you accomplish your goals and aspirations—and to determine whether or not you are achieving them. Defining your goals & aspirations should be the starting point for your improvement initiative; every meaningful activity in which you engage should be dictated by a goal or set or goals that you are trying to accomplish or aspirations that you are trying to achieve. To put it in roadmap terms, the goal is the destination, and once you know where you are trying to go you can then define the best route to get there. If you do not know where you are going, then you can never find the route to get there. So, you either end up wandering aimlessly or staying in the same place you are today—miserable and unfulfilled.

The concept of "strategy" (or planning) can be confusing, so I developed a model to help simplify the concept and to make it easier for laypersons to understand, embrace, and engage with. The model I developed is referred to as The **G.O.A.T.** (GOAT). I developed the GOAT model—**G**oals, **O**bjectives, **A**ctivities & **T**asks—to help people articulate & develop goals and aspirations (business, professional, and personal) and the activities necessary to achieve these goals and aspirations. Before proceeding, a few definitions are necessary.

GOAL

A goal is the specific intended result of an activity or a set of activities in which someone is engaged. It answers the questions: Why am I engaging in these activities or making changes in my life? What am I trying to accomplish? A goal is a general statement of an intended outcome and it takes the form of an action statement: "**To [action verb] [noun]**". For example, a woman who is trying to lose weight might be doing so because she wants "to look good" for her 20-year high school reunion. In this example, the woman's goal (aspiration) might be defined as: "I want to look 'good' for my high school reunion"—however she defines "good." Another example might be a real estate agent whose goal is "To become the top real estate agent in Los Angeles"—however "top" is defined; more on that later.

In his book *Flourish: A Visionary New Understanding of Happiness and Well-being*, psychologist Martin Seligman argues that genuine well-being comes from promoting five elements of well-being: pleasure, engagement, relationships, meaning, and achievement—also known as P.E.R.M.A. *Pleasure* is, simply put, feeling good. *Engagement* is associated with having a good, full life comprised of satisfying work, close *relationships* with family and friends, and interesting hobbies. *Meaning* refers to feeling that you are part of a larger purpose; *Meaning* and *Achievement* are consistent with Maslow's Self-Actualization need. While all elements of well-being are important, they are not equally important. Seligman believes *engagement* and *meaning* are most crucial for a happy life. **Goals give people a sense of purpose**; they **give life meaning**. They provide people with hope, optimism about the future, the confidence to pursue that which is possible, and the motivation to grow, develop, and better themselves and their station in life; goals give many people a reason to live. When a person successfully accomplishes a goal that he or she has defined for themselves, they not only realize the benefits that accompany successful goal accomplishment (e.g. being the top real estate agent in Los Angeles), but they also gain the motivation to strive to be even better. In doing so, they move that much closer to satisfying the need for Self-Actualization and becoming truly fulfilled in life.

OBJECTIVE

An objective supports the goal. It answers the question: What specific thing(s) must I accomplish or achieve so that I will know that I have accomplished my goal? A simple rule-of-thumb for articulating desires as objectives is to ask two questions about the desires: **"How much?" and "By when?"** So, if you want to "increase my income," in order to convert this subjective desire into a measurable objective, you should ask "By [how much] would I like to increase my income?" and "[By when] would I like to have my income increased to that level?" You might then re-articulate your aspiration as a measurable objective, such as "I would like to increase my income by $10,000, before December 31, 2015."

There should be no ambiguity or wiggle room when it comes to determining whether or not a person has accomplished an objective. Objectives should be "S.M.A.R.T."— Specific, Measurable, Attainable, Realistic, and Time-bound.

- **Specific**: It should be clear to anyone reading the objective exactly what you are trying to do. And if 100 people read the objective all 100 people would have the same understanding of what you are trying to accomplish or achieve;

- **Measurable**: Objectives should be so specific and quantifiable that you know without a doubt whether the objective has been achieved or not—because you can measure your results related to the metrics. If you define an objective "to eat 20 hot dogs in less than 5 minutes," at the end of the 5-minute period, you will know without a doubt whether or not you successfully ate 20 hot dogs;

- **Achievable**: Achieving the objective should be possible— even if difficult—within your desired timeframe, given the resources available to you. If you defined an objective to eat 200 hot dogs in 5 minutes it would be a poorly-defined objective, because it would not be humanly possible for you to achieve this result;

- **Realistic**: An objective can be achievable, yet unrealistic. For example, if you set an objective to eat 90 hot dogs (and buns!) in 10 minutes, the feat would be possible, but unrealistic; the 2014 Nathan's Hot Dog Eating Contest (an annual American competitive eating competition) crowned repeat champion, Joey Chestnut, who devoured 69 hot dogs (and buns) in 10 minutes;

- **Time-bound**: Objectives should be defined so that they can be achieved within a timeframe that adds a sense of urgency, importance, and gives you an opportunity to reap the benefits from achieving them.

Following the example of the person who wants to become Greater Los Angeles's top real estate agent, she might learn that to achieve this, her closed transaction volume for the year would have to exceed $161 Million. Armed with this knowledge, the real estate agent might define an objective as: "To become the top real estate agent in Los Angeles (the goal), I must sell $162 Million in closed transaction volume by December 31, 2014." Since the real estate agent knows the sales number she would have to attain "To become the top real estate agent in Los Angeles," if she actually does exceed that target number and sells the $162 Million that she defined as her objective (target), she will have, in turn, accomplished her goal.

And the woman who is trying to lose weight because she wants "to look 'good' for her 20-year high school reunion" (her goal)? She might define her measurable objective as: "I want to lose 15 pounds over the next 30 days," because she believes that if she does so, she will look "good" and, therefore, will have accomplished her identified goal for the high school reunion—which is only 30 days away. This implies, of course, that the only thing the woman needs to do to look "good" is to lose weight. If true, then achieving her objective of losing 15 pounds would result in goal accomplishment. If she finds, however, that losing the 15 pounds is not enough to make her look "good," then achieving her weight-loss objective would not result in goal accomplishment. As a result, she would need to re-define what it takes to look "good," and possibly develop a second objective (such as: "To save $500 over the next 30 days and purchase a fabulous dress—and shoes!—to complement my new figure"). **Ensuring that the successful achievement of your specific objectives results in the successful accomplishment of your associated goal is critical.** Objectives should be defined using "if-then" logic: if I do "A" and "B," then "C" will be the result. For example, if (A) I lose 15 pounds within 30 days and (B) I save $500 to buy a dress and a pair of shoes (my objectives), then (C) I will look "good" for my high school reunion (my goal). A way to validate the strength of the objectives you define toward the accomplishment of the goal they support is to follow a process (which is described below).

Scenario: Ken is on the track & field team. He is a sprinter who competes in the 100-meter dash (109.4 yards). The fastest sprinter on Ken's team is James, whose best time in the 100-meter race was 10.8 seconds. Because of this time and the fact that James can squat 200 pounds of weight (greatly strengthening his thighs and gluteus muscles, giving him more speed—in addition to giving him locker room bragging rights), James is considered the fastest runner on the team; Ken wants to be considered the fastest.

1. Define your goal or that to which you aspire (e.g. I want to be the fastest runner on my team);

2. Define the performance metrics (objectives) that, if achieved, will make you the fastest person on the team (1. Complete the 100-meter race in under 10.8 seconds; 2. Squat more than 200 pounds of weight; and I want to accomplish both feats within 12 months);

3. Validate that by achieving the objectives, you will have succeeded in accomplishing your goal. (If I can run a sub-10.8-second race and squat more than 200 pounds, I will best James' team records and I will then be considered the fastest runner on the team; I will have accomplished my goal).

The Relationship Between Goals and Objectives

GOAL

To be the fastest runner on my track team

OBJECTIVE 1

Complete the 100-meter dash in under 10.8 seconds; within 12 months

OBJECTIVE 2

Squat more than 200 pounds of weight; within 12 months

These two objectives are well defined because if Ken achieves both feats, he will be considered the fastest runner on his track team; he will have accomplished his goal.

ACTIVITIES & TASKS

After you have established a goal and the associated objectives that quantitatively and specifically define the goal and its accomplishment, the next step is to do something to accomplish the objectives and, consequently, the goal. This introduces the **Action Plan** concept.

An *action plan* is a guide for how you will accomplish an objective and the associated goal. It answers the question: What specific initiatives, activities, action items, and/or tasks must be completed to accomplish the associated objective? For the woman whose objective is to lose 15 pounds in 30 days, she might determine that she must begin a weight-loss regimen (the initiative or **Activity**) that requires her to jog one mile per day (a **Task**) and to consume fewer than 1,700 calories daily (a task). By following this weight-loss regimen, the woman will lose the 15 pounds within the 30-day window thereby accomplishing her objective, which will make her look "good" for the reunion—her goal.

So, if the woman follows a weight-loss regimen and successfully loses 15 pounds within the next 30 days, while also working overtime so she can save $500 and purchase the dress and a pair of shoes, then the combination of the weight loss, the fabulous dress, and the new shoes will help make her look "good" for the high school reunion. At that point, the woman will have successfully accomplished her goal. That accomplishment will make the woman feel better about herself and her achievement. As a result, she will gain more confidence—not only because of her improved physical self, but also because she knows that she can accomplish whatever she puts her mind to—and, most importantly, she will move a step closer to Self-Actualization and being the best that she can become.

GOAL: To look "good" for my 20-year high school reunion	
Objective 1 in Support of the Goal	**Objective 2 in Support of the Goal**
To lose 15 pounds over the next 30 days	To save $500 over the next 30 days to purchase a fabulous dress—and shoes!—to complement my new look
Activity to Achieve Objective 1	**Activity to Achieve Objective 2**
Begin a weight-loss regimen (the Activity)	Work one extra hour of overtime per day (so that I can earn the extra $500)
• Task 1: Consult my physician	• Task 1: Get approval from my boss
• Task 2: Join a fitness gym	• Task 2: Rearrange my calendar
• Task 3: Purchase a Thigh-Master	• Task 3: Save "sale" coupons from Macy's
• Task 4: Purchase running shoes	
• Task 5: Buy earphones	
• Task 6: Find a jogging trail	
• Task 7: Jog one mile each day	
• Task 8: Research low-calorie meal recipes	
• Task 9: Consume less than 1,700 calories per day	
• Task 10: Throw away all "junk" food	
• Task 11: Purchase a blender	

PLAN EXECUTION

The #1 reason why plans and strategies fail is because of poor plan execution. It is not enough to simply *want* to change; you must also *make* the changes necessary to accomplish your goals and aspirations. In other words, you must *execute* your plan or strategy. **Execution** means accomplishing the necessary tasks and action items to complete the defined activities and achieve your objectives. It means doing the things that you have outlined in your plan as the things you need to do to improve your life. In the example about the woman who wants to look "good" for her high school reunion (represented in the table above), she defined two necessary activities to accomplish her objectives (Activity #1: Begin a weight-loss regimen; and Activity #2: Work one extra hour of overtime per day so that she can earn an extra $500) and 14 different tasks necessary to execute the activities. By completing (executing) the 14 Tasks that lead to the successful completion of the two activities, the woman will (hopefully) achieve the two objectives which will result in goal accomplishment. Without completing the 14 Tasks, the woman will not lose the desired weight or earn the additional money necessary to achieve her objectives, preventing her from accomplishing her ambitious goal.

The "Cause-and-Effect" Nature of a Plan or Strategy

Effective plans/strategies contain relationships that follow the cause-and-effect logic, ruling out coincidence as much as possible. Cause-and-effect supposes that if you do "A" then

"B" will happen as a direct result of "A." If you do not do "A," however, then "B" will not happen.

Coincidence, on the other hand, supposes that if you do "C" then "D" happens. However, "D" could have happened even if you did not do "C." Therefore, the "D" event would be considered a coincidence, because it randomly happened right after you did "C," and its occurrence was not related to or caused by the "C" event.

An example of causation (cause-and-effect) is turning on a light switch: when you flip a light switch, the light comes on. If you flipped the switch 100 times, the light would come on 100 times. The light coming on (the effect) is a direct result of you having turned on the light switch (the cause for the light coming on). And it is safe to assume that, if you did not turn on the light switch, then the light would not go on. Another example of cause-and-effect related to the example of a woman who wants to look "good" for her high school reunion can be seen below:

To look "good" for my 20-year high school reunion		
Objective 1	**Cause of the Weight-Loss**	**Effect of the Weight-Loss Activities**
To lose 15 pounds over 30 days, which the woman accomplished	Began a weight-loss regimen: • Task: Jogged one mile each day • Task: Consumed less than 1,700 calories daily • Etc.	The woman lost weight, because she effectively executed her weight-loss regimen.

In this example, the cause-and-effect relationships between the elements of the woman's plan/strategy exist as described in the diagram below.

The Cause-and-Effect Relationships
Between the Elements of a Plan

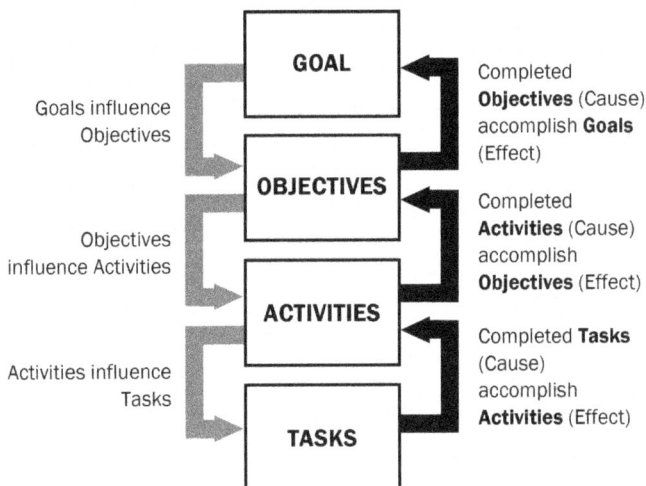

Goals influence Objectives

Completed **Objectives** (Cause) accomplish **Goals** (Effect)

Objectives influence Activities

Completed **Activities** (Cause) accomplish **Objectives** (Effect)

Activities influence Tasks

Completed **Tasks** (Cause) accomplish **Activities** (Effect)

GOAL

OBJECTIVES

ACTIVITIES

TASKS

An example of a coincidence, on the other hand, is if you wore your lucky socks to two baseball games and each time, your favorite team won the game. The act of wearing your "lucky" socks to the baseball games had nothing to with the team's victories. Only a crazy person would believe that his or her socks caused that to happen.

The "if-then" nature of planning and strategy holds that once we undertake an action, we expect that the outcome of the action (an outcome we predicted would occur before we took the action) actually occurs. If it does, then we consider the next action in which to engage that will get us another step closer to achieving an objective and/or accomplishing a goal.

ADJUSTMENTS

The quantitative and/or measurable nature of objectives enables you to determine whether or not you are making progress toward achieving your objectives and accomplishing their associated goals. This is a good thing, because, as you measure your progress, if you find that you are not making improvements or getting closer to achieving your objectives, you can modify the necessary plan elements to get back on-track.

A plan should be a "living" document. As such, it should be continually monitored, edited, and updated as necessary based on the conditions that surround you and the factors that impact plan pursuit. Plans and strategies are expected to be modified over time, so when you find that it becomes necessary to make plan adjustments do not panic; every successful plan or strategy that I have ever developed for a company, organization, or individual—and I have done hundreds globally—has been modified at some point. Plan adjustments should not always be seen as something negative. If, for instance, after measuring your progress toward achieving a plan objective you find that you are way ahead of schedule, then adjusting the plan to reflect the fact that you are doing so well is great; it means that you will begin reaping the rewards of an accomplished goal sooner than originally hoped.

The Improvement Model: A Summary

Element	Description
Acknowledgment	Before any meaningful improvement can be made to a person's condition, station, or performance, there must be acknowledgment (an admission, recognition, and acceptance) that "something" in the person's current state is unsatisfactory to the *person* and/or not meeting the person's expectations or aspirations.
Identification	Acknowledgment and acceptance that "something" in your current state is unsatisfactory to you and is not meeting your expectations/aspirations is the first step toward becoming better. The next step is identifying that unsatisfactory "something" so that you can then begin to address it.
Genuine Desire to Change	Improvement is about making changes that will lead us in a "new direction;" all improvements require change. For change to happen in your life, you, and only you, must be ready and willing to make the necessary changes to achieve your aspirations.
A Plan	A "Plan" is a "Strategy" and a Strategy is a Plan. Whichever term is used, they both can be considered a road map for getting you from point-A to point-B. By definition, a strategy is a plan to achieve objectives—measurable targets that have been established to help you accomplish your goals and aspirations, and determine whether or not you are achieving them.

Adjustments	A plan should be a "living" document. As such, it should be continually monitored, edited, and updated as necessary based on the conditions that surround you and the factors that impact plan pursuit. Plans and strategies are expected to be modified over time, so when you find that it becomes necessary to make adjustments to the plan do not panic.

THE RELATIONSHIP BETWEEN THE MODEL FOR IMPROVEMENT AND THE THREE STAGES OF IMPROVEMENT

As a refresher, the **Three Stages of Improvement** are the stages that people go through when attempting to improve from some initial, undesired state to becoming the best that they could become.

Stage 1: Dissatisfaction. A person in the Dissatisfaction stage finds him/herself in an undesired state, which results in unhappiness, disappointment, and/or non-fulfillment.

- When dissatisfied, one must first acknowledge and accept that s/he is not perfect and/or is dissatisfied with some aspect of her/his life before s/he can move toward improvement;

- Once the person has acknowledged her/his un-fulfillment, s/he must then try to identify the reasons for the lack of fulfillment and dissatisfaction as the next stage in the improvement process.

Stage 2: Enlightenment. A person progresses into the Enlightenment stage when s/he accepts her/his current circumstance as a part of life, understands the reason(s) for her/his dissatisfaction, and envisions & believes there is a way forward to measurable, significant improvement.

- A person starts to become enlightened once s/he begins to understand the reasons for her/his discontent and realizes the need to make changes in her/his life. S/he then commits to making the changes necessary to improve her/his situation or condition;

- As the person begins to develop a plan or strategy for making the necessary improvements in her/his life, the person can then begin to execute elements of the plan. As s/he does so, the person will be on the path toward improvement and becoming their best selves possible—Optimization.

Stage 3: Optimization. After a person has progressed from her/his state of dissatisfaction and becomes enlightened through self-acceptance and hope, s/he then defines a path forward which s/he follows. As s/he follows the path, s/he begins to make gradual improvements in her/his life to become the best person that s/he can be and to perform at the highest level at which s/he is capable; this highest level of capability is the Optimization stage.

- As the person executes Improvement Plan elements and makes necessary adjustments to the plan, the person will start to make improvements in her/his life as well. The more of the plan the person executes, the more improvements the person will make until, ultimately, the person will have accomplished her/his goals and realized her/his aspirations.

The Relationship Between the Model for Improvement and the Three Stages of Improvement

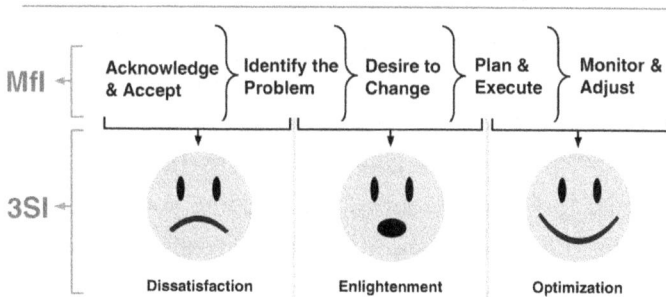

| | Acknowledge & Accept | Identify the Problem | Desire to Change | Plan & Execute | Monitor & Adjust |

MfI

3SI

Dissatisfaction   Enlightenment   Optimization

THREE TIPS FOR CREATING A BETTER G.O.A.T.

As you develop your personal Improvement Plan, here are three suggestions to make your planning efforts as sensible as possible.

1) **Practice restraint when establishing your goals**. A plan should ideally have no more than three (3) goals to be accomplished. The process of pursuing and successfully achieving the multiple objectives that may be associated with a single goal can be very time-consuming and even challenging. If you are pursuing "too many" goals (more than three, or definitely more than five), then you are

actively not trying to accomplish any of them. It's like going on a 2-day trip to Paris, France: your to-do list might contain twenty things to see and do over the course of the two days which, you will soon realize, is not enough time to truly appreciate any of them. The result will be that you will leave Paris frustrated at the fact that you couldn't accomplish all of the items on your list, as opposed to appreciating the fact that you spent two days in Paris.

A single, short-term goal (one that is expected to take between 6 and 12 months to accomplish) can take up more than a year of your available free time. A long-term goal (36 to 60 months) can become your occupation. The more goals you attempt to accomplish, the more time it will take and the less motivated you will be to continue pursuing them. For these reasons, I recommend that your initial Improvement Plan consist of one or two short-term goals (ideally, goals that can be accomplished within one year). As you begin to execute your plan, the improvements you start to make will motivate you to work even harder at accomplishing the goals.

2) **Answer the three Improvement Questions**. As you begin the process of developing your plan's GOAT, answering the following questions will help you better define the goals & aspirations, objectives, and activities & tasks.

- *What are you trying to accomplish*? The answers to this question will help you articulate your **goals**. The goals are your aspirations; they are the things that, when all is said and done, you want to be, become, accomplish, and/or achieve.

- *How will you know that a change is an improvement?* The answers to this question will help with articulating and crafting your **objectives**. Objectives should be quantitative and/or measurable so that there is no doubt whether you have achieved them or are progressing toward the achievement of your improvement objectives.

- *What changes can you make that will result in an improvement?* The answers to this question will help with determining and crafting your **activities and tasks**. Task completion should lead to (cause) the accomplishment of activities (a/k/a/ initiatives and projects); completion of activities should lead to (cause) the achievement of your objectives; and the completion of your objectives should lead to (cause) the accomplishment of your associated goal.

3) **Ensure that cause-and-effect relationships exist between the elements of your plan's GOAT**. Check for cause-and-effect relationships between the Tasks and Activities; the Activities and Objectives; and the Objectives and Goals. If a cause-and-effect relationship does not exist between *every one* of your plan's GOAT elements, then you should either re-define the elements that do not have a relationship with an associated element or remove the elements all together.

7

Developing *your* Improvement Plan

THE 7-STEP IMPROVEMENT PLAN PROCESS

[To make the Improvement Plan development process easier for you, I have made all forms and tools referenced in this section available for free download from my website www.TabEdwards.com or www.Imperfekt.Me]

It is impossible to understand how to get where you are going if you do not *know* where you are going. To make improvements in your life, you must have a vision of where you would like to go, what you would like to achieve, what you would like to become, and how you see your life at some future point. You must be able to imagine your ideal self if ever you are to become it.

Far too often, people pay lip service to making improvements in their lives ("When cigarettes hit $5 per pack [as they did back in 2008], I am going to quit smoking!"). Every year millions of people make New Year's resolutions that fall by the wayside when we attend our company New Year's buffet luncheon or by February 1st, whichever comes first. We make these resolutions because we acknowledge that some aspect of our lives could be "better" or that we are unsatisfied with something in our lives and want to make improvements. The challenge for most of us is that *damned* buffet luncheon, or the smell of cigarette smoke, or that paycheck we receive every two weeks, or that paycheck we no longer receive, or that needy child, or that spoiled child, or that comfort of being with a loser as opposed to being alone, or that competitor who outcompeted us, or that competitor we couldn't outcompete, or that party at Tri Delta Sigma, or that beer at Tri Delta Sigma, or that string of five football games on television Sunday, or that alarm clock that we hate to hear at 6:00AM, or those opinions of other people, or that irrational expectation of perfection that we have of ourselves, or that house we cannot sell because it is under water, or that house we cannot afford to buy, or that school tuition we struggle to pay, or that student loan following us around, or that glass ceiling we were afraid of breaking, or that senior who clutches her purse when we get on the elevator, or that side of the tracks where we don't belong, or that unaffordable cost of basic healthcare, or that lack of food and decent shelter available to us; we always seem to find things that prevent us from achieving what we want to achieve or becoming what we want to become.

Some challenges that we face when hoping to make life improvements are simply excuses ("I can't study for my exam tonight—in hopes of improving my grades—because there is a wild party going on at Delta Sigma Theta") and some are genuine obstacles ("I cannot find a mailing address to use so that I can get a job"). The improvement planning process is about identifying that to which you aspire and figuring out a way to overcome the obstacles you will inevitably face along the way toward achieving that aspiration or accomplishing your desired goals.

Over the years I have developed a 7-Step process—which I call **The 7-Step Improvement Plan**—designed to help people make improvements in their lives, accomplish their desired goals, achieve their aspirations, and become the best that they can. The 7-Step Improvement Plan ("Improvement Plan") follows the proven process that I have used with organizations, businesses, and people around the world to help them make the changes necessary for improvement. The 7 Steps are presented below.

STEP #1: ACKNOWLEDGE THAT YOU WOULD LIKE TO IMPROVE SOME ASPECT OF YOUR LIFE

Before any meaningful improvement can be made in a person's condition, station, or performance, there must be an acknowledgment (an admission, recognition, and/or acceptance) that "something" in the person's current state is unsatisfactory to the *person* and/or not meeting the person's expectations or aspirations.

Answer the following questions

Is there an aspect of your life that you would like to be "better" or that you are dissatisfied with?	**YES**	**NO**
Is your level of accomplishment or performance in some aspect of your life unsatisfactory to you, at a level that you consider disappointing, or below some standard that you have defined or aspire to?	**YES**	**NO**

If you answered "Yes" to either question, continue on to the next step.

STEP #2: IDENTIFY THE REASONS WHY YOU ARE UNFULFILLED OR WOULD LIKE TO MAKE IMPROVEMENTS IN YOUR LIFE

The acknowledgment and acceptance that "something" in your current state is unsatisfactory to you and is not meeting your expectations/aspirations is the first step toward being better. The next step is identifying that unsatisfactory "something" so that you can then begin to address it. This activity will help you understand the things that bring you displeasure and the reason why you are experiencing them.

Answer the following Issue Identification Questions (IIQs)

IIQ #1	What bothers you about yourself, your situation, your level of performance, and your level of achievement? What are you unhappy with or dissatisfied about? [List all of the things you can think of]
IIQ #2	What would a "fixed" problem or an "improved you" look like, feel like, perform like, or achieve? [Create a list of all of the items you can think of]
IIQ #3	What do you want to change and improve, or believe you need to change or improve? [Create a list of all of the items you can think of]
IIQ #4	What is the difference between you today and the "you" you want to become? [List the all of the visions of the "you" you want to become. List all of the differences between you today and the "you" you want to become]
IIQ #5	What are the possible reasons why people in your undesirable situation are in the situation which you find yourself? What did you learn from your past experiences, the similar experiences of others, and the feedback loop about why you are in the current unsatisfactory position in which you find yourself? [List all of the reasons you can think of]

Combine the list of items you created from the Issue Identification Questions above into two groups:

- **Group #1—Improvements Needed**: Responses from Issue Identification Questions #1, 2, 3, and 4. Rank the list of items from #1 (the most critical, significant, or desirable issue to address or improve) to the last item (the least important or most insignificant issue).

- **Group #2—Reasons for Your Current State**: Responses from Issue Identification Question #5.

Match Improvements Needed (Group #1) with Reasons for the Condition (Group #2)

From your lists, match the unsatisfactory issues in your life (Group #1) to the reasons why the unfavorable conditions that you want to change exist (Group #2).

STEP #3: VISUALIZE YOUR IDEAL SELF AND CONDITION. VISUALIZE THAT TO WHICH YOU ASPIRE. BE WILLING TO MAKE CHANGES IN YOUR LIFE.

Perfection is in the opinion of the relevant receiver; there is no absolute standard or agreement on what is considered to be perfect. The only perfection that matters is "your perfection," defined as being the best "you" possible and accomplishing all that you can accomplish, even if it is short of becoming a deity. What is "your perfection?" Imagine it; visualize it.

There is a link between thoughts and behaviors; you must be able to visualize what you aspire to in order to realize it. You must also visualize the positive benefits that will befall you should you make changes. This will motivate you to not only *desire* change, but also to make the changes necessary to improve your life.

To begin the process of visualizing, it is helpful to consider your answers to the questions below. Your answers to these questions will not only help you to visualize and imagine a better state of being, but will also serve as the foundation for defining the things to which you aspire—your personal Goals.

Answer the following Visualization and Change Questions

1	What is "your perfection," your aspiration(s)? What does it look like? [Describe all of the versions that you can think of]
2	What would your life be like if you could achieve your aspirations? [Describe all of the visions that you can think of]
3	If you could change only one thing about your life what would it be? Why would you want to make that change? [Repeat this process to identify the top 3 things you would want to change]
4	Why do you want to be "better"? [List all the reasons you can think of]
5	Would you be happy and personally fulfilled if you did nothing, and kept things exactly the way they are today? If not, why not? [List all the reasons you can think of]

6	Other than the fear of "uncertainty," what is preventing you from making changes to improve your life? [List all the things you can think of]
7	Are you willing to make changes in your life or are you 100% satisfied with your life as it is today?
8	Are you willing to work at becoming better even if the changes you need to make do not happen overnight?
9	How will you avoid trying to change the things you cannot control, and focus on changing those that you can? [Describe it]
10	During the process of making changes in your life, it is important to reward yourself for small accomplishments. How will you reward yourself as you make progress with your change efforts? [List all the ways that you can think of]

Combine the answers you created from the Visualization and Change Questions above into two groups:

- **Group #1—Your Aspirations**: Responses to Questions #1, 2, 3, 4, and 5. Rank the list of items from #1 (the most critical, significant, or desirable aspiration or vision) to the last item (the least important, least desirable, or most insignificant aspiration or vision).

- **Group #2—Inhibitors to Change**: Responses to Question #6.

Best Practice

To visualize your "best" or ideal self, try this: Imagine yourself as you would like to be; your ideal. Imagine your accomplishments, your job, your partner, your relationships, your income, your home, your health, your appearance, your knowledge, your surroundings, your acquaintances, and imagine your ideal world. What does it look like? Are you happy in your visualized world? Now, describe these things in one or two paragraphs.

Next, eliminate those things that you visualized which are impossible to achieve—not *difficult*, but impossible. Then, rank the remaining things that you visualized (e.g. your job, your income, your appearance, your health, etc.) in order of desirability; item #1 should be the thing that is most desirable to you.

After that, list the differences between the items you visualized for yourself and your actual self. For instance, if your visualized job was an "attorney," and your current real job is an administrative assistant, what are the differences between where you are today and becoming an attorney? List them all. Do this for each item you visualized. These "differences" will help you determine the activities you need to accomplish to achieve the realistic aspirations you visualized (goals).

STEP #4: DEVELOP THE GOALS TO YOUR IMPROVEMENT PLAN

Using the lists you created for the groupings "Group #1: Improvements Needed" from Step #2 above, and "Group #1: Your Aspirations" from Step #3 above, create a combined list of all the items in both groupings and re-rank them from #1 to #N. This list will become your "Potential Goals" list. From the list of Potential Goals, select the top-10 ranked aspirations or visions (Potential Goals).

Fine-tune the list of 10 Potential Goals

Before going forward with this process, it is necessary to ensure that the Potential Goals are properly articulated as goals, and that the goals follow the format **"To [Action Verb] [Noun]."** Some examples of action verbs include: reduce, increase, improve, establish, develop, become, stop, etc. Some examples of simply-defined goals include: "To [grow] the [revenue] in my small business 500%"; "To [become] [debt] free"; and "I want to [look 'good'] for my [high school reunion]."

The definition and format of the goals (as well as the objectives) is important, because it allows you to easily establish a relationship between goals and objectives; it allows you to create cause-and-effect relationships between them; and it is a standard format, which means that anyone who is familiar with strategic planning can review the plan and understand exactly what it means.

To revise the top-10 list of Potential Goals and get them into the proper format, do the following for each of your list's 10 Potential Goals:

1. Work to identify the "real" goal you hope to accomplish or the "real" aspiration you hope to achieve. This can be done by subjecting each Potential Goal to the following filtering process:

   A. Write the Potential Goal as you have captured it

   B. Ask this question about the Potential Goal: "Why do you desire that [Potential Goal]?

   C. If your answer to this question cannot be taken further (as illustrated in the diagram below) or it does not make sense, then the way you have written the Potential Goal is ready to take to step (2). If, however, your answer to the question can be taken further as illustrated in the diagram below, then THAT answer becomes your re-defined Potential Goal. For example, if your Potential Goal was "to alleviate my back pain," the reason you want to do it is obvious and it cannot be taken further with an answer to the question. However, if your Potential Goal was "to be handsome," the reason why you want to be handsome is not obvious, so whatever the reason (such as, "I want to find a partner"), that reason will become the "real" Potential Goal—or, at a minimum, it will get you closer to defining what you really want to achieve —and should be re-written.

1	**2**	**3**
Perceived Aspiration	**Reason(s) Why Desired**	**The Real Aspiration or Goal**
"To be Handsome" (Ambiguous)	"To Find a Partner" (Practical)	**"To Find a Partner,"** (NOT "To be Handsome")

2. Structure and re-write each "real" Potential Goal into the proper format as necessary: **"To [Action Verb] [Noun]."**

3. Choose the one or two most critical, important, desirable re-written Potential Goals from your top-10 list; these will become the goals you will pursue via your Improvement Plan.

Best Practice

A brainstorming technique for identifying possible goals, desires, and aspirations is to create a "wish" list. By developing a wish list, you will uncover the foundation for various goals to which you aspire. When the wish list is developed, you can then re-write them in the proper form of a goal. You can start by using this wish list idea template. Complete the following sentences.

"I wish I _____"

"I wish I could _____"

"I wish I didn't _____"

"I wish I was _____"

"I wish I had _____"

For instance: "I wish I had a college degree" could be converted into the goal: "To [earn] a [bachelor's degree] from Temple University."

STEP #5: DEVELOP THE OBJECTIVES FOR YOUR IMPROVEMENT PLAN

An objective supports the goal. It answers the question: What specific thing(s) must I accomplish or achieve so that I will know that I have accomplished my goal? A simple rule-of-thumb for articulating desires and aspirations as objectives is to ask two questions about the desires and aspirations: **"How much?" and "By when?"** So, if you aspire to "increase my income," in order to convert this subjective desire into a measurable objective you should ask "By [how much] would I like to increase my income?" and "[By when] would I like to have my income increased to that level?"

For this activity, select one (1) of the goals you defined in Step #4 to use throughout this objective-definition activity.

Create a list of Potential Objectives for your chosen goal

Using the list of answers to Issue Identification Question #4 (from Step #2 of this process) and Question #1 from the Visualization and Change Questions (from Step #3), identify potentially quantifiable and measurable responses. For each of these responses, ask "How much?" and "By when?" and create a list of answers; these entries will become part of your "Potential Objectives" list. For example, if one of your answers to IIQ #4 was "The difference between the me today and the me I want to become is financial wealth," by asking "How much wealth would satisfy your financial wealth problem and by when would you hope to earn that amount?" you might create a measurable Potential Objective: "I want to earn $50,000 annually within the next 18 months." The same process would apply to your answers to the Visualization and Change Question.

Note your answer to IIQ #4 from Step #2

IIQ #4	What is the difference between you today and the "you" you want to become? [List all of the visions of the "you" you want to become. List all of the differences between you today and the "you" you want to become. **Refer to the Best Practice at the end of Step #3**]

Note your answer from the Visualization and Change Question from Step #3

1	What is "your perfection," your aspiration(s)? What does it look like? [Describe all versions that you can think of. **Refer to the Best Practice at the end of Step #3**]

Answer the following questions based on your chosen goal

1. How will you be able to definitively measure/determine that you have accomplished your goal? [Your answer(s) and the metrics you define will be added to your Potential Objectives list]

2. What quantifiable or measurable accomplishments will you need to achieve to confirm that you have successfully accomplished your goal? [In the example of Ken, the track & field athlete, Ken wanted to be considered

the fastest runner on the team. To do so, he defined the performance metrics (objectives) that, if achieved, would give him the distinction of being the fastest person on the team: Complete the 100-meter race in under 10.8 seconds and squat more than 200 pounds of weight, and he wanted to accomplish both feats within 12 months].

3. How will engaging in the action that will result in the measurable accomplishments referenced in question #2 get me closer to accomplishing the goal?

4. Determine the measurable, quantitative differences between you today and the "you" that you visualized. These differences should become Potential Objectives.

5. Does a cause-and-effect relationship exist between my list of Potential Objectives and my chosen goal? If so, list them.

Your responses to these questions will contribute to your brainstormed Potential Objectives list.

Objectives should be S.M.A.R.T. Using the checklist below, validate that your defined objectives that support goal #1 are SMART.

Is each objective Specific?	**YES**	**NO**
Is each objective Measurable?	**YES**	**NO**
Is each objective Achievable?	**YES**	**NO**
Is each objective Realistic?	**YES**	**NO**
Is each objective Time-bound?	**YES**	**NO**

If you answered "no" to any of the above questions, re-structure and re-write the objectives so that they are properly formatted (answers the questions "How much and by when?") and SMART.

Link each potential objective to your chosen goal

At this point in the process, you should have created a list of potential goals and a list of potential objectives for your Improvement Plan. The next task is to match the goals to their related objectives. **Remember**: Objectives should be related to a specific goal (there can be multiple objectives associated with one goal and vice-versa), and your achievement of the objectives should result in the accomplishment of the related goal. In the example of Ken the track & field athlete, Ken's goal was "To [be] the [fastest runner] on my track team." Related to that goal were two objectives: (1) Complete the 100-meter race in less than 10.8 seconds; and (2) Squat more than 200 pounds of weight, within 12 months. The relationship between Ken's goal and his two objectives was the following: If Ken accomplished both objectives, then he would be the fastest runner on his track team; he would have accomplished his goal. This is illustrated in the diagram below.

The Relationship Between
Goals and Objectives

GOAL

To be the fastest runner on my
track team

OBJECTIVE 1	OBJECTIVE 2
Complete the 100-meter dash in under 10.8 seconds; within 12 months	Squat more than 200 pounds of weight; within 12 months

These two objectives are well defined
because if Ken achieves both feats, he
will be considered the fastest runner on
his track team; he will have accomplished his goal.

So, if one of the goals on your Potential Goals list was
"To become a practicing attorney in the state of New Jersey,"
your matching objectives—the measurable achievements
needed to accomplish your goal of becoming an attorney—
might be: (1) "To complete the degree requirements (credits
and courses) for a Juris Doctor (JD) degree within 3 years";
(2) "Pass the New Jersey Bar exam with a 155+ scaled MBE
score within 2 years after receiving my JD degree"; and (3)
Land a job with a New Jersey law firm within 6 months of
passing the Bar exam." In this example, earning a JD degree,
passing the bar exam, and getting a job as an attorney would
mean that you had accomplished your goal of becoming a
practicing attorney.

Best Practice

A method of effectively completing the goal-to-objective matching process is to select the first goal (e.g. "To become a practicing attorney in the state of New Jersey") and then find the objectives (from your potential objectives list) that relate to the goal AND that would lead to goal accomplishment if the objectives were achieved.

Ensure that there is a cause-and-effect relationship between the objectives and the goal: If the objectives are achieved, the result will *unquestionably* be the accomplishment of the associated goal.

STEP #6: DEVELOP THE ACTIVITIES AND TASKS NEEDED TO ACHIEVE THE OBJECTIVES

The activities portion of your plan is where specific projects, initiatives, and general activities that lead to objective achievement are defined. This is where "difference-reduction" activities become helpful, because the differences between the "you" today and the "you" that you want to become indicate different activities that must be completed (differences reduced) to achieve your objectives and accomplish your goals.

For example, if your goal is "To become a practicing attorney in the state of New Jersey," and one of your related objectives is "To complete the degree requirements (credits and courses) for a Juris Doctor (JD) degree within 3 years," then the activity/initiative and the associated tasks that must be finished for you to complete the JD degree within 3 years become the differences between you today and you with a JD degree (within 3 years). It might look something like the table below:

Goal	To become a practicing attorney in the state of New Jersey
Objective #1	To complete the degree requirements (credits and courses) for a Juris Doctor (JD) degree within 3 years
Activity & Tasks (to achieve the objective)	Activity 1: Take the Law School Admission Test (LSAT) • Task: Take an LSAT preparation course • Task: Register for the exam Activity 2: Apply to law schools • Tasks: (List them) Activity 3: Enroll in a law school • Tasks: (List them) Activity 4: Get into a good study group at the law school • Tasks: (List them) Activity 5: Others • Tasks: (List them)

Identify the activities needed to achieve your objectives

After linking your potential objectives to your chosen goal, it is then time to determine the activities that must be completed to achieve your objectives and the tasks that must be completed to accomplish the activities.

For each goal-objective pairing, answer the questions presented in the table outline below. This format attempts to clearly present the relationships between the goal, the goal's supporting objectives, the related activities to the objectives, and the tasks related to the activities. You can create your own table or use one from the website (recommended).

Goal	Objective	Activity	Tasks
Your chosen goal	The objective that supports the goal	The activities that achieve the objective	The tasks that must be completed to accomplish the activity
What is Goal #1?	What are the objectives that support Goal #1?	What are the activities that support each objective?	What are the tasks that support each activity
Goal #1	Objective #1	Activity #1	Task 1
			Task 2
			Task 3
		Activity #2	Tasks 1
			Task 2
			Task 3
Goal #1	Objective #2	Activity #1	Task 1
			Task 2
			Task 3
		Activity #2	Tasks 1
			Task 2
			Task 3

Cause-and-effect logic should still apply: Completed tasks lead to completed activities; completed activities lead to achieved objectives; achieved objectives lead to accomplished goals.

**The Cause-and-Effect Relationships
Between the Elements of a Plan**

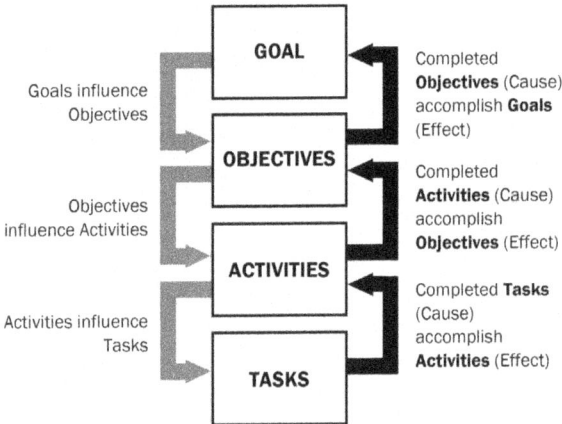

Does a cause-and-effect relationship exist between your list of Potential Objectives and the chosen goal? Validate the relationships.

Combine all of the Goals, Objectives, Activities, and Tasks into a first draft of your Improvement Plan

Congratulations! You are well on your way to making improvements in your life toward becoming better at whatever your pursuit. Once your Improvement Plan is cleaned up a bit, you can then begin to execute the plan and realize the benefits of making positive changes.

Best Practice

To determine the activities / initiatives that must be developed and completed to achieve an associated objective, ask the following question: From my current station in life, what are all of the things that must be done for me to achieve that objective?

STEP #7: EXECUTE THE PLAN, MONITOR YOUR PROGRESS, AND MAKE ADJUSTMENTS AS APPROPRIATE

Plan "execution" is about *doing* something; it is about completing the plan's activities and tasks ("action plans") by specified completion dates that relate to the desired completion date of the associated objective. To facilitate the process of executing and tracking progress with your Improvement Plan, the use of a **Scorecard** is recommended.

A Scorecard is a plan management tool that lists all of the objectives, activities/initiatives, and tasks that are part of your plan, and presents the data in an easy to follow format that not only shows you what needs to be completed by when, but also gives you an at-a-glance reference of how you are progressing with the completion (execution) of your plan. A Scorecard template is available through my website www.TabEdwards. com, as are all the forms necessary to complete your Improvement Plan. A sample Scorecard is provided below.

SAMPLE SCORECARD

Goal: To Look "Good" for my 20-year High School Reunion

Objective #1	Status	Resource Needed	Owner	Due Date
To lose 15 pounds over the next 30 days	On-Track			09.30.2015
⋀ **Begin a weight-loss regimen (Activity #1)**	On-Track			08.31.2015
• Task 1: Consult my physician	On-Track	N/A	Me	08.15.2015
• Task 2: Join a fitness gym	Completed	Money for the fee	Me	08.25.2015
• Task 3: Purchase a Thigh-Master	On-Track	Mom's old Thigh-Master	Me	08.31.2015
• Task 4: Purchase running shoes	Not Started	Money for the cost	Mom	08.29.2015
• Task 5: Buy earphones	Not Started	Money for the cost	Me	08.29.2015
• Task 6: Find a jogging trail	Completed	N/A	Me	08.29.2015
• Task 7: Jog one mile each day	Not Started	N/A	Me	08.30.2015
• Task 8: Research low-calorie meal recipes	Not Started	Brother's support	Brother	08.25.2015
• Task 9: Consume less than 1,700 calories daily	Not Started	N/A	Me	08.31.2015
• Task 10: Throw away all "junk" food	Behind	N/A	Me	08.25.2015
• Task 11: Purchase a blender	On-Track	Money for the cost	Me	08.25.2015

The "Action Plan" portion of your Improvement Plan (the activities, tasks, task owners, resources needed to complete the tasks, and the expected completion dates of each task) defines WHO ("owner") will do WHAT ("task") by WHEN ("date").

Element	Description	Owner	Date
Goal	To become a practicing attorney in the state of New Jersey		
Objective #1	To complete a Juris Doctor degree within 3 years		
Activity & Tasks	Activity 1: Take the Law School Admission Test	Joan	12.31.15
	• Task: Take an LSAT preparation course • Resource: Money to pay for the course • Resource: Kathy to help me prepare	Joan	12.31.14
	• Task: Register for the exam • Resource: Money to pay for the registration • Resource: Bob's PC so I can register online	Joan	06.30 15

It is important to remember that the due dates or completion dates for each task should align with the desired completion date of the objective they are in support of. For instance, if the objective is expected to be achieved within six months, the tasks (and the associated activity) must be completed within a timeframe that will allow the objective to be completed by its desired achievement date.

Monitor your progress and make adjustments to the plan as necessary

Using your Scorecard, track your progress periodically (I recommend at least weekly) to see how well you are accomplishing the tasks in your plan within the timeframe that the tasks are expected to be completed. If you are on-track executing your plan, then reward yourself; you will have earned it. If, however, you are falling behind schedule, make adjustments to the plan as necessary (whether it is adjustments to the tasks, due dates, or resources needed to complete the tasks) to get you back on-track.

The risk of falling behind in your plan's execution is the possibility that objective completion could be delayed or stalled and, therefore, the accomplishment of your goals could also be delayed, stalled, or even worse, fail. Such a delay—whether it is a delay completing tasks, activities, or objectives—means that there will be a corresponding delay receiving the benefits of having accomplished your goals and making the desired life improvements.

Best Practice

Reward yourself for making progress toward your goal. For example, after you have completed an Activity (or, depending on the difficulty, a Task), give yourself a small reward. While small, these rewards motivate you to continue with what can at times be a challenging Improvement Plan.

Although I recommended that you use only one goal the first time you follow this process, The 7-Step Improvement Plan should be repeated to include each of the goals that you identified as being desirable or necessary for you to be happier and more fulfilled. In the end, you will have a completed Improvement Plan—complete with Scorecards—that includes all of the important goals you have established for yourself. As you begin to successfully accomplish your goals, you will become more fulfilled, happier, and motivated to accomplish your other goals, too. Each time you do, you will get one step closer to becoming the best you possible.

8

Five Guiding Principles *for* Leading *a* More Enjoyable, Fulfilling, *and* Less Miserable Life

PRINCIPLE #1
FIND YOUR PASSION AND PURSUE IT

A person's **"passion"** in this context is the thing that inspires the person to want to immerse him/herself in a topic or activity. It is the thing that makes us want to get up every day so that we can engage in it. It is our feeling for the thing that we simply love to do, regardless of how often we engage in it. Our passion is that which drives us, which motivates us, which gives us a sense of purpose. Our passion is the thing that excites us, that makes life enjoyable.

There is a saying that the person who loves his job never works a day in his life. For those people, their passion is their work. What is your passion? Is it your profession? Is it your hobby? Is it the quest for knowledge? Is it spirituality? Is it physical fitness? Is it writing? Is it reading? Is it cooking? Is it eating? Is it charity? Is it simply "living"?

One of the reasons I have found for why people have not found their passion is because they simply do not know how to determine what their passion is or what it could be. When I work with people who have a desire to improve their lives and we discuss their passion, I have found that the easiest way for people to identify their passion is to (A) follow Step #3 of **The 7-Step Improvement Process** (Visualize Your Ideal Self and Condition. Visualize That to Which You Aspire) and/or (B) answer my "long-lost uncle" question which reads as follows: Imagine that you received notification that you had a long-lost uncle whom you don't even remember; the uncle has passed away. When you were a baby, the long-lost uncle thought you were the most precious thing in the world and has left you $10 million in his will with one condition: you cannot use the money to travel the world and take a lifetime vacation; you must do some productive work—even if it is turning your hobby into your profession. Simply put: you can do anything that you want or have ever wanted to do without concern about earning a living. What would you do? The answer to that question can help you define your passion.

[Here's an interesting factoid: Out of the hundreds of times I have asked this question (excluding to entrepreneurs and charity workers), only one person—ONE—has ever said that she would continue to work at her current job; everyone else said that they would quit their jobs *immediately*. This sheds some light on why so many people are miserable: they are working in jobs that they dislike so much that, if they had the opportunity to quit their jobs "immediately," they would do so].

The pursuit of and engagement in one's passion gives life meaning and inspires us to achieve greater heights and do greater deeds. People often say that the pursuit of their passion not only gives life meaning, but also gives them a sense of feeling *valued*. When people feel valued, our sense of self-worth increases and we begin to see ourselves in a better, more significant light, which increases our feelings of self-worth, self-esteem, and even self-confidence. I have found this to be true for me personally, too. I have always had a passion for helping the less fortunate, probably because I grew up among the less-fortunate. I am grateful that the ball bounced in my favor a few times and I am, therefore, fortunate enough to have a roof over my head and food on the table; but this is, sadly, not the case for far too many people. When I help people who really need help, it makes me feel good. It makes me feel like I am doing something worthwhile which gives me a sense of having some modicum of value in the world. No: it is not my speeches, my seminars, my coaching, or my business dealings that provide me with this fulfillment; it is often that brief, yet subtle, smile, that inviting expression on weathered faces that says "I appreciate you"—no words need be spoken. No public recognition needed. No "thank you" due. We follow our passions for our own intrinsic reasons, not because they have been externally-dictated. For that reason, they have more personal meaning for us.

Once you have identified your passion, I recommend that you make the pursuit of that passion one of your Improvement Plan goals. You will be glad you did.

PRINCIPLE #2

FORCE YOURSELF TO BE HAPPY, WHETHER YOU LIKE IT OR NOT

Let's face it: many of us *make* ourselves unhappy even when we have the option of not doing so. We often get so caught up worrying about what other people think of us, putting the welfare of others before our own, believing that it is "better to give than to receive," and feeling responsible for the happiness of others at the risk of our own comfort, that we feel guilty about doing things for ourselves. Eventually, the normative behavior becomes sacrificing our own enjoyment to make other people happy and to persuade our neighbors to think highly of us. Stop it!

To be truly happy, you have to take responsibility for your own happiness; don't rely on others for *your* personal happiness. If you do, then your happiness is randomly based on the consideration and whims of others, which means that your happiness is a crap-shoot and out of your control. You want to go to the movies to see the midnight showing of "Nosferatu" but your husband doesn't want to go? Forget him; go by yourself. You want to take a vacation to Disney World to check out the new Fantasy Land expansion, but your kids hate Disney World? Then leave the spoiled brats at home and go to Disney World by yourself! You want to attend the annual Flower Show but your boyfriend is allergic to flowers and, therefore, doesn't want to go? Call your back-up, second-string date, leave your Allegra*-sniffing loser of a boyfriend at home, and go smell the roses. You want to wear your Sly Stone silver platform disco boots but you're afraid that your neighbors will ridicule you? Try this: put on the boots, walk outside, go over to your neighbor's house, knock on their door, and when they answer, tell them to kiss your ass! You have to do the things that *you* decide are in your self-interest if you want to be happy and fulfilled. You have to become responsible for your own happiness and fulfillment.

I know it's hard to behave this way when you have a family or other loved ones who rely on you for *their* happiness, well-being, and support. But you must force yourself to be happy and not feel guilty about doing things because of what others will think or what you might be "taking away" from other people. Your enjoyment and fulfillment is not a zero-sum game where the only way you can do things that *you* want to do is if someone else gets slighted; you must change that mindset. But how, you might wonder?

Below I have provided some recommendations of things that work wonders for the people I work with to improve their lives and to help them become happier and more fulfilled. While these recommendations are not complex, they have proven to be extremely effective. To quote one individual who followed this prescription: "I was sort of surprised that these simple, no-brainer ideas actually work quite well. Having done them, I am definitely having more fun and I am happier than I have been in quite some time."

The following is a prescription that you can follow to help you transform that "guilty" mindset and get on the path to happiness.

Create a "Guilty-Pleasure List"

By calling it a "guilty pleasure" list, you are acknowledging that it is a list of things that you would normally feel guilty about doing, even though they will (hopefully) bring you pleasure. And the more you look at your Guilty Pleasure list, the less power and impact the word "guilty" will have on your psyche and, eventually, you will begin to disassociate the activities on your list with this nagging, annoying feeling. I liken it to the word "geek." Prior to the late 1990s dot-com boom, being called a "geek" was quite an insult. It implied that a person was un-cool, nerdy, dorky, a dufus bookworm who carried pens in a pocket protector. But with Internet expansion, "geeks" started developing Internet-based services & companies, netting themselves millions of venture-capital and Initial Public Offering (IPO) dollars in the process, and catapulting themselves to rock-star status (does anyone really think that Facebook's Mark Zuckerberg is traditionally cool?). Suddenly, it became cool to be a geek, and now nerdy, smart people everywhere are proud to wear that label.

By creating a Guilty-Pleasure List, you seize the opportunity to stop living vicariously through other people and start becoming the person you want to be by doing the things you've always dreamt about doing. Creating the list is not only fun, but it's also easy to do. First, brainstorm and write down a list of everything that you've ever wanted to do. One way to help generate ideas is to consider this hypothetical question: If you knew that you were going to die tomorrow, what things would you look back on and regret not having done, experienced, or accomplished? Add those items to your Guilty-Pleasure List (as well as your list of Possible Goals). As you brainstorm, don't worry about how much money the activity will cost, what your neighbors or family will think, the possible trade-offs associated with you engaging in the activity, or how selfish or how guilty you will feel; just create a laundry list of things that you want, have ever wanted, or might want to do in the future. Once you start your list, you will probably realize how much you are and have been missing out on by not acting in your own self-interest and doing some of the things on your list.

Next, rank order the items on your list based on how badly you want to do them—disregarding how much it will cost, what people will think of you, how neglected your family will be, or how guilty you will feel. So, if your Guilty-Pleasure List consists of 50 activities, the activity that you want to do more than any other would be rated #1 and the activity you would want to do last would be rated #50. After creating and ranking the items, only *then* consider such things as feasibility and any potential negative impact on other people or yourself. Remove any items that you determine to be untenable, unachievable, and/or selfish (negatively impacting other people), then re-rank the items.

Once your Guilty-Pleasure List has been edited and re-ranked, make it a priority to do at least one thing from your list each and every month without fail.

Create a monthly Do Diddly Day

A *Do Diddly Day* is a total blow-off day where nothing is planned or structured. It is a day for *you*; a day to do whatever you want to do on your own terms and without any external influences, family responsibilities, or household chores. Your wife wants to go to the in-laws on your Do Diddly Day? Tell her you'll take a rain check. Your kids need a ride to the soccer game? Tell 'em to walk. Remember: this is *your* day and whatever you decide to do on your Do Diddly Day—even if you decide to do *nothing*—will be determined by you and you alone based on your own intrinsic motivation.

To make the best use of free time and your Do Diddly Day, you must devote as much creativity and attention to it as you would to your job. Active leisure not only helps you grow as a person, but also leads to higher levels of enjoyment in an activity.

Initially, when you inform your family and friends that you are having a Do Diddly Day, you might receive feedback from them that you are "selfish," "inconsiderate," or "lazy." For the Do Diddly Days to work, you have to block out these distractions and condition yourself to not succumb to external pressures and to not feel guilty about doing something for yourself. Something you can think about to make it easier to ignore feedback from others is this: when your family and friends ask you to sacrifice *your* happiness so that you can make *them* happy, THEY are the ones who are being selfish; you are being self-interested, and there is a difference.

Selfish vs. Self-Interest

As I wrote in my book *Chocolate Peppers: Why acting in your own self-interest is good for you, your loved ones, society, and the world*, two terms that are often interchanged and misconstrued are "selfish" and "self-interest." Contrary to what you may have learned, the two words have completely different meanings.

To be selfish is to be concerned almost exclusively with oneself and one's own advantage, pleasure, or well-being; and this is the key point: *without regard for other people*. Selfish-acting people inconsiderately engage in selfish behavior; the only thing that matters to a selfish person is their own pay-off; everyone and everything else be damned! If the selfish peanut butter-sandwich-lover wants to have a sandwich but doesn't want to eat alone, he will coerce his peanut-allergic-girlfriend into eating a peanut butter sandwich, too, just so that he can have company. And the likelihood that the self-ish peanut butter sandwich lover's innocent girlfriend will become sick as a result of his coercion? "Too bad," would be the selfish person's response.

There was an award-winning Broadway play by Lorraine Hansberry entitled "A Raisin in the Sun," which became a major motion picture in 1961 starring Sidney Poitier. It is a story about a family living on the South Side of Chicago whose matriarch becomes the beneficiary of a $10,000 life insurance payment. The family is conflicted over how to use the money, money that would afford the family many op-tions to get ahead in life. One of the family members, Wal-ter Lee, wants to go into business with friends who plan to open a liquor store. So, unbeknownst to the other family members, Walter Lee selfishly invests the money into the liquor store and eventually loses it all. Walter Lee acted self-ishly because he invested the money in a risky business venture without regard for the interests of (or consequences for) other family members.

Selfish people cultivate *egocentrism*, believing that the world revolves around them and is there simply to serve their interests and desires. The behavior of selfish individuals—whether the behavior is purposeful, accidental, or unconscious—is often detrimental to others, suggesting that, for selfishness to occur, other people must be involved. If Fred went to the bank and withdrew his family's entire life savings just so he could light it on fire since he likes the smell of burning money, his actions would undoubtedly be considered selfish. However, if Fred was the last surviving person on earth and he went to the bank and withdrew his family's entire life savings for the same reason, would that be considered selfish? I say, no, because Fred's actions would have *no impact on anyone else*; there would be no negative consequences of his actions, because no one would care. And if Fred's actions couldn't negatively impact other people or himself, then his actions would be considered self-interested; the difference is the involvement of other people.

Self-interest is integral to personal survival. It is in our self-interest to have food and shelter. It is in our self-interest to exercise and take care of our health. It is in our self-interest to have a job and earn enough money to support basic needs. Self-interest is an essential component of our overall sense of well-being. Self-interest—satisfying one's needs—is not mutually exclusive from caring for others.

The table below helps illustrate the subtle differences that can exist between that which is selfish and that which is self-interested.

An Example of "Selfish"	An Example of "Self-Interest"
When stranded in the sweltering heat of the desert with a friend, drinking the last remaining bottle of water by yourself so that **you** can stay alive.	When stranded in the sweltering desert with a friend, drinking half of the water in the bottle so that you **both** can stay alive.

Having a Do Diddly Day—a day to yourself, a day to act completely in your own self-interest, unencumbered by any type of responsibility whatsoever—is healthy and often mentally needed. Taking a monthly Do Diddly Day will make you happier throughout the year, enabling you to spread happiness to other people at least once per month. Psychological research has shown that happiness is more strongly correlated with the *frequency* of satisfying events rather than with the intensity of these events. So, if you are happy more times than you are not, then, overall, you will live a happier life which will benefit you and others, too; a monthly Do Diddly Day will force you to be happy at least twelve times per year ... whether you like it or not.

Continue to learn new things and gain new experiences

When we learn new things and gain new experiences, we open ourselves up to a whole new world of possibilities and opportunities for gratifying experiences that were unknown to us in our previously "closed" state. As we learn new things and gain new experiences, we will inevitably discover new activities that provide us with not only knowledge, but also fulfillment … so much so, that we engage in these new experiences with such intensity that we lose ourselves in them, even to the point where we lose track of time. Have you ever engaged in an activity—gardening, reading, cooking, painting—that was so engrossing that hours passed like minutes and, were it not for the interruption of life's other responsibilities, you could have continued even longer? That is the promise of learning new things: we gain experiences and discover new activities that contribute to our additional happiness and fulfillment.

Psychologist Mihaly Csikszentmihalyi, the author of *Finding Flow*, refers to the condition in which people are so intensely absorbed in a task that they lose track of time and place as "Flow." According to Csikszentmihalyi, flow generally occurs when a person is *actively engaged* in a favorite activity, such as mountain biking, for example. It can also occur when driving, talking to friends, and even at work. Very rarely do people report flow in passive leisure activities, such as watching television or simply relaxing. He also states that the happiness that follows flow is of our own making—in other words, it is based on the choices we make out of our own intrinsic choices *based on our self-interest*.

Lifelong learning can improve your self-esteem and help you live a fuller, richer, and healthier life. By continuing to learn, you can develop a greater understanding and breadth of knowledge in things that interest you, increasing the likelihood of finding new passions, learning new skills, and developing new hobbies that bring you happiness and improve the richness of your life. Learning new things—which can also be included in your list of Possible Goals—can help keep your mind sharp and promote well-being; it can also be a social outlet and a form of entertainment, thus further expanding your options for happiness.

PRINCIPLE #3

DEVELOP AND EXECUTE AN IMPROVEMENT PLAN

In *Chapter 7: Developing Your Improvement Plan*, I presented **The 7-Step Improvement Plan** as a process for making improvements in your life working toward accomplishing your goals and becoming the best that you can become. Developing and executing an Improvement Plan is one of the most sure-fire ways to improve the quality of your life and be happier and more fulfilled.

Enjoy the journey

Some people become so intensely-focused on achieving the objectives and goals of their Improvement Plan that they neglect to appreciate the many pleasures that progress offers. For these people, the end result is the only benefit and the process of getting there is simply a distraction. This is like going to the super-exclusive New York City restaurant, Masa (with its $300-$500 prix fixe menu), ordering a delicious meal, and not enjoying the sensory pleasure that each bite of food brings; the only reason you are eating the food is to get it into your stomach so that you are no longer hungry. Don't eat such a meal to simply satisfy your hunger, but savor the meal. Enjoy the process of eating delicious food. Enjoy the tastes and smells and texture and visual presentation of the food sitting before you, for doing so will not only make the experience a more pleasurable one, but will also help you enjoy accomplishing the goal (eliminating hunger) even more.

Enjoy the journey and the pursuit of achieving your goals. If your goal is to lose 20 pounds to become healthier, celebrate the first five pounds lost, then ten, then the fifteenth lost pound. Each weight-loss milestone will bring with them a modicum of happiness, because you have achieved some success; and success breeds happiness. Successfully-achieved milestones will also bring a sense of accomplishment and self-pride (and a bit more happiness) because you are succeeding in the pursuit of a healthier you. There is value in the journey, so embrace it. You cannot maximize your potential or achieve your lifelong goals in one fell swoop; the only way to get there is to start by being better than you are today—one task at a time, one milestone at a time.

PRINCIPLE #4

DO NOT LET OTHERS DEFINE YOU OR YOUR ACTIONS; DEFINE THEM FOR YOURSELF

As referenced previously, the poet Audre Lorde once stated:

"If I didn't define myself for myself, I would be crunched into other people's fantasies for me and eaten alive." A great sentiment if ever there was one. What Lorde suggests by this statement is that people should feel free to be who they intrinsically want and choose to be, and they should not let other people determine that role for them. The consequences of allowing other people to define you include the potential for them to use you however they choose. To them, you are what they want you to be and, since they have placed you in a particular role, they have the right to do with you what they will.

Another expression of being defined by others is when you derive your happiness from the happiness that you provide others, even if it means your own happiness comes second. People who are anxious to please others by fulfilling their needs and expectations are called "People-Pleasers." People-pleasers thrive on the praise, adulation, and positive response they receive from the people they spend so much effort to please.

According to Linda Tillman, a psychologist at Emory University, people-pleasers are unable to gauge the value of their own actions, and "As a result, they spend their lives looking for validation from others." I think it is sad when a person believes that "If I don't please this person or these people, they will not like me." This behavior eventually becomes self-reinforcing, making the behavior difficult to change. The pattern of feeling valuable only by complying with others' demands can lead a person to lose sight of their own personal aspirations, leaving the people-pleaser to live an unfulfilled and even miserable life.

To be happy and fulfilled, we cannot be bullied by other people or controlled by external influences, especially when it is in our own self-interest to do otherwise. In making decisions about your life and your happiness, consider only what your heart and mind covet. You only get one shot at this life so you can't let anyone dictate the course of your life, except you. Other than when you were a child, have you ever trusted anyone enough to allow them to make life-choices on your behalf and believed they could make better choices than you could? Probably not. You, and only you, know what's truly in your heart and what you desire most in this world.

Do not conform to a way of thinking or behaving that other people define for you because you are concerned what they will think if you do not conform. No one should create your identity or dictate your world view; that's your responsibility. Rational people should neither allow this nor allow anyone to chart the course of their life. If you do, then you are in a cult. Get out!! Remember: It is your life, and *you* must define yourself for yourself … or risk being eaten alive.

Don't Define Yourself Compared with Others

The idiom "Keeping up with the Joneses" refers to how people use their neighbors' material positions and social status as the benchmark to measure themselves and their social standing. For some people, not keeping up with the Joneses means that they are existing below some acceptable standard of wealth, status, or even equality—standards dictated by the Joneses and not by you.

By measuring yourself against the accomplishments, wealth, and status of other people, you are allowing them to indirectly define you. I believe that when you measure your station against other people, you are acknowledging that you are disappointed with your own station in life. Why does the fact that your neighbor drives a Mercedes Benz and you drive a Yugo make you feel inferior? Because it reminds you of just how cheap and inferior your car is and how relatively poor you are; it shouldn't, but it does. Why does it bother you that your neighbor hires a professional landscaping company to groom his lawn and you have to cut your own grass using a 14-inch, manual, $79 Economy Reel Mower? Because it reminds you of how cheap your mower is … and how much less money you have; it shouldn't, but it does. And why on earth does the fact that your neighbor vacations in the Hamptons and you can only afford to go to Wildwood, New Jersey for the day irk you? Because it makes you feel as though you have underachieved in life; it shouldn't, but it does.

It's okay to admire someone's achievements and even aspire to reach those heights yourself. That's different than measuring yourself against other people and believing that, in order for you to no longer feel like a loser, you have to match their accomplishments, wealth, and status. That type of envy and overly-wanting what you don't have can lead to jealousy and resentment, two emotions that contribute to misery; and obviously, when you are miserable, you are not happy.

Don't resent anyone else's success, looks, wealth, or achievements, either. Doing so won't improve *your* situation; it'll only make you miserable. Being jealous or envious is an expression of the disappointment you feel regarding your own progress, so, if anything, you should be angry at *yourself* instead of jealous of the other person. Once you recognize that your jealousy doesn't help *you*, you can then focus on fixing your perceived shortcomings by, for instance, following The 7-Step Improvement Plan.

So acknowledge other people's success, give them credit for their accomplishments, but aspire to do the best that you can and strive to achieve as much as you are capable of achieving. When you do this, it will become easier to accept that you are the best person that you can be and that your life is not defined by other people.

PRINCIPLE #5

AVOID FALLING INTO MISERY TRAPS

To begin the quest to lead a more enjoyable, fulfilling, and less miserable life, one must first understand how to avoid being miserable; this requires an understanding of why miserable people are miserable and how they became that way. If, for example, you wanted to know how to make a delicious cake, it would be helpful to know and avoid the pitfalls that cake-bakers experienced when their baking resulted in low quality, bad-tasting cakes. The same is true with enjoyment: If you want to know how to enjoy life and become more satisfied, it would be useful to identify the pitfalls of being miserable first so that you can avoid them.

Psychologist Jeffrey Bernstein, who has worked on this subject with individuals, couples, and families for more than twenty years, believes there are two reasons why people become miserable: (1) Desperately wanting what they don't have; and (2) Desperately NOT wanting what they already have—with an emphasis placed on *desperately*. Bernstein argues that aspiring to achieve goals in life beyond our current station is healthy, but aspiring to goals that are ridiculous and unachievable can lead to misery.

For example, Billy is a 21-year-old college senior who plays on his school's junior varsity basketball team. He is 5'9", cannot dunk the basketball, is a 60% free-throw shooter, and has not been able to crack the starting lineup for his Division III basketball team. Billy's lifelong goal—a goal he has aspired to since he was 8 years old—is to play professional basketball in the National Basketball Association (the NBA); not the NBA's Development League (D-League), but the fully-fledged NBA. Barring some miracle, such as Billy waking up one morning and finding he has miraculously morphed into Dirk Nowitzki, it's not happening. Billy lacks the talent or physical attributes to play professional basketball and his irrational pursuit of a NBA career will lead to frustration, resentment of those who have achieved the

NBA, hopelessness, and general unhappiness, leading him to become miserable.

Overly not wanting what one does have is similar to overly wanting what you don't have, but there are subtle differences. In the example of Billy the basketball player, although Billy does not have the talent to play in the NBA, it's possible he has the talent to play professional basketball at some level; there are lots of "professional" basketball leagues around the country, many of which—with his size and talent level—Billy could play in. But Billy doesn't want his current talent level; he wants LeBron James's which means that, as long as he holds this lofty aspiration, he will remain miserable. Meanwhile, there are thousands of aspiring basketball players who would love to have Billy's talent and be able to play at the Division III collegiate level. If Billy could come to grips with the fact that he will never play basketball in the NBA but that he could still play professional basketball in other leagues, he could gain satisfaction and enjoyment from the game he loves.

Being miserable is awful, but, because "misery loves company," when we are miserable, we also bring others down into our pit of resentment, hopelessness, and general unhappiness. But if we become aware of what makes people miserable (and therefore, unhappy), we have a better chance of avoiding these "misery traps," and improving our prospects for being more fulfilled. To help in this effort, I have provided some common misery traps and their associated misery-avoidance tips in the table below.

Misery Trap	Misery Avoidance Tip
Thinking negatively and being pessimistic	Focusing on possibilities rather than limitations; it'll open up opportunities you might not have otherwise discovered.
Being jealous of other people and resentful of everything	Not defining yourself by others or evaluating your life's journey relative to others. Define yourself for yourself. Appreciate what you are and what you have.
Wasting too much effort trying to change the things or people you cannot change	Focusing on changing the things you can change; it'll reduce your feelings of hopelessness.
Focusing on problems and life's challenges	Focusing on the post-problem state, defining a way to get there, and relishing life's possibilities.

Misery Trap	Misery Avoidance Tip
Considering your station in life (if you are unhappy with it and unfulfilled) to be permanent	Defining a realistic vision of what you would like your station to be and developing a GOAT to figure out how to get there.
Doing non-mandatory things for others at the expense of acting in your own self-interest	Following the recommendations in Principle #2: Forcing yourself to be happy whether you like it or not.
Hanging out with other miserable people	Acquiring new friends.
Assuming that you are always right and that your way is the only way	Guess what? You're not and it's not! Continuing to learn, associating with knowledgeable people, and seeking truth. Be honest with yourself and acknowledge that no one—not even you—is always right; you will open the door to recognizing when you are wrong and beginning to value the contributions of others.
Holding grudges unnecessarily	Holding a temporary grudge is not necessarily a bad thing, depending on the circumstance. But eventually, you have to forgive or resolve or eat the loss, and eventually forget.
Simply living day-to-day with nothing that sparks a passion	Finding a passion and diving in head-first. It will help give life meaning.

CONCLUSION

I use the word "Imperfekt" to represent an acknowledgement that we are imperfect and there is an opportunity for us to be better than we are today. No person, place, or thing is perfect, so if you have aspirations of being perfect or achieving perfection in some endeavor, you should come to this realization and accept that you will never accomplish or achieve it. The best that we can aspire to and hope for is to continually improve our lives, to be better than we are today in achieving our highest potential, to becoming our "best" selves, and to strive for Self-Actualization. Therein lays our "perfection."

I am sure that some readers will say that we should always pursue perfection, because even if we fall short of that goal, we will have made improvements in the pursuit of perfection. This is not invalid. I, too, agree that there are benefits in the pursuit of perfection. The problem occurs with people who are "neurotic perfectionists" and can never be satisfied with their performance or the specific stage of excellence that they have achieved. For these people, the pursuit of perfection ceases to become a process for improvement, but instead becomes an unachievable obsession, relegating the people to constant misery, disappointment, and unhappiness.

An issue on which I disagree is that perfection is a rational goal to pursue; it is not. To pursue perfection as a goal, in and of itself, is to pursue a myth or that which does not exist. Only a psychopath would do such a thing, not a rational person. The goals that we pursue should be realistic and attainable, even if not easily accomplished. This is supported in The 7-Step Improvement Process where the person developing the Improvement Plan must ensure that his or her aspirations are realistic and achievable. S/he must also ensure that the objectives s/he pursues (objectives that indicate the successful accomplishment of their goals) are "SMART": Specific, Measurable, Attainable, Realistic, and Time-bound; "perfection" is none of these things.

If there is such a thing as perfection, then I believe it is that which a person defines as "perfect" for him or her; it does not mean that their vision or definition of perfection will be agreed upon by anyone else. But does it matter that no one else acknowledges that what you define as "your perfection" is what they will also agree is perfect? It should not matter, because, in the end, the only perfection that matters is "your perfection," even if "your perfection" is nothing more than a personal goal or aspiration that you want to pursue and achieve to become the best "you" possible. In my opinion, THAT definition of "your perfection" is, in fact, your "perfection."

ABOUT *the* AUTHOR

TAB EDWARDS is an Amazon.com bestselling author of ten books and is considered one of the most brilliant, creative, engaging, and entertaining speakers in the country. He has worked with thousands of people and organizations around the world to become more effective at accomplishing their goals and "better" at their pursuits.

Tab's workshops, coaching sessions, seminars, and speaking engagements are highly regarded and have been delivered to general audiences and professionals at organizations around the world, including: IBM Corporation, AT&T, Pfizer, Cigna, FannieMae, Hewlett-Packard, Staples, Towers Perrin, Haliburton, Drexel University, Penn State University, Citigroup, and the global AIIM (Association for Information and Image Man agement) Conference, to name just a few.

SPEAKING REQUESTS

TAB EDWARDS is available for various speaking engagements, including: motivational, seminar, keynote, and custom-tailored addresses. These engagements are guaranteed to be both fun and inspiring.

To book Tab for a speaking engagement or to request more information, please visit us at www.TabEdwards.com or feel free to send an e-mail message to info@TabEdwards.com.

SPEAKING ENGAGEMENTS, SEMINARS, AND KEYNOTE ADDRESSES

Inspiring Audiences

Tab Edwards is a master presenter whose speaking engagements have been described as "Incredible!", "Motivating!", "Fun as well as inspirational," and "Wow!"

Tab believes that audiences should not only be able to absorb a presenter's message and be able to apply it in the real world, but they should also be inspired to go out and do so immediately after hearing a presenter speak. Audiences attend presentations and seminars to learn new things that they can apply to various aspects of their lives in hopes of making improvements, and they are also there to be engaged and entertained. Tab Edwards is considered one of the most engaging, entertaining, and impactful speakers in America.

Motivating Teams

Sales seminars, meetings and conventions should be inspiring, entertaining, and informative, to motivate professionals to higher levels of achievement. Anything short of this will leave audiences feeling as though their time could have been better spent elsewhere; that is not the objective. Tab Edwards is prepared to deliver a keynote speaking engagement that will motivate your team to higher levels of performance and provide them with useful information, while doing so in an entertaining and uplifting manner.

Tailored, Audience-Focused

Many seminars and speaking engagements are canned, one-size-fits-all endeavors in which the presenter simply delivers the content that he or she wants to deliver, with very little opportunity for appropriate tailoring. Tab's approach is different. He begins the process with an understanding of what the host wishes to accomplish through the seminar, and—together—Tab and the host craft an agenda that best accomplishes the seminar's goals.

For those clients that prefer to receive suggestions for seminar content based on the popularity and success of content delivered at Tab's other engagements, he offers a variety of proven seminar options to fit most every meeting theme.

ADDITIONAL INFORMATION

If prompted for a password when downloading
the Plan Forms from the website
www.TabEdwards.com or www.Imperfekt.Me
enter 'cupcake' (lower case letters)

Follow Tab Edwards on Twitter:

@TabAuthor

Selected Bibliography

"1945 Baron Philippe De Rothschild Chateau Mouton Rothschild, Pauillac, France." Wine Searcher. <http://www.wine-searcher.com/win-127-1945-baron-philippe-de-rothschild-chateau-mouton-rothschild-pauillac-france>

"25 Worst Performing Public Schools in the U.S." *DailyFinance.com*. <http://www.dailyfinance.com/photos/worst-performing-public-schools/>

"3 Reasons He Didn't Call You Back." *www.marieclaire.com*. Marie Claire, 7 Apr. 2009. <http://www.marieclaire.com/sex-love/advice/why-he-didnt-call>

"31 Places to Have the Perfect Beach Vacation." *CondÁ Nast Traveler*. Conde Nast Traveler, 19 Feb. 2004. http://www.cntraveler.com/galleries/2014-02-19/best-beach-vacations-hawaii-mexico-bahamas

"487. Very Important Diamond." Sotheby's, 13 May 2014. <http://www.sothebys.com/en/auctions/ecatalogue/2014/magnificent-jewels-noble-jewels-ge1402/lot.487.html>

4Cs Brochure. Gemological Institute of America Inc., 2014. http://gia4cs.gia.edu/media/pdf/LAB_4cs_brochure_US_English.pdf

"52 Perfect Movies: Citizen Kane (1941)." Cinema Geek, 16 Feb. 2010. <http://cinema-geek.blogspot.com/2010/02/52-perfect-movies-citizen-kane-1941.html>

"60 Minutes/Vanity Fair Poll: The Perfect Man." *CBSNews*. CBS Interactive, 8 July 2013. <http://www.cbsnews.com/news/60-minutes-vanity-fair-poll-the-perfect-man/>

"Absolutism vs. Relativism - Is Truth Subjective?" *ValME*. 20 July 2014. http://valme.io/c/philosophy/cmqqs/absolutism-vs-relativism-is-truth-subjective/

ACT. *Assessment technical manual*. ACT. (1997). Iowa City, IA.

"ACT History." ACT, Inc. <http://www.act.org/aboutact/history.html>

Alk, Nell. "Emily Blunt on How She Overcame Her Stutter."*www.vulture.com*. Vulture, 8 June 2011. <http://www.vulture.com/2011/06/emily_blunt_stuttering.html>

"American Film Institute." *AFI's 100 Greatest American Movies of All Time*. American Film Institute, 16 June 1998. <http://www.afi.com/100years/movies.aspx>

The American Heritage Dictionary of the English Language, Fourth Edition copyright ©2000 by Houghton Mifflin Company. Updated in 2009. Published by Houghton Mifflin Company.

Antony, Martin M., and Richard P. Swinson. *When Perfect Isn't Good Enough: Strategies for Coping with Perfectionism*. Oakland, CA: New Harbinger Publications, 1998.

Aten, Emily, and Rachel Masters. "Public Opinions About Stuttering."*www.mnsu.edu*. Minnesota State University, n.d. <https://www.mnsu.edu/comdis/kuster/journal/hallen/public.html>

Benson, Etienne. "The Many Faces of Perfectionism." *Http://www.apa.org*. American Psychological Association, 1 Nov. 2003. <http://www.apa.org/monitor/nov03/manyfaces.aspx>

Bernstein, Jeffrey. "Liking the Child You Love." *Psychology Today*. December 18, 2010. http://www.psychologytoday.com/blog/liking-the-child-you-love/201012/the-two-real-causes-misery

Bernstein, Richard J. *Beyond Objectivism and Relativism Science, Hermeneutics, and Praxis*. Philadelphia: U of Pennsylvania, 1983.

Blatt, Sidney J. "The Destructiveness of Perfectionism: Implications for the Treatment of Depression." *American Psychologist* 50.12 (1995): 1003-020.

Blatt, Sidney J., David C. Zuroff, Colin M. Bondi, Charles A. Iii Sanislow, and Paul A. Pilkonis. "When and How Perfectionism Impedes the Brief Treatment of Depression: Further Analyses of the National Institute of Mental Health Treatment of Depression Collaborative Research Program." *Journal of Consulting and Clinical Psychology* 66.2 (1998): 423-28.

Bourg Carter, Sherrie. "Why We Dread (and So Often Fail To) Change."*www.psychologytoday.com*. Psychology Today: Health, Help, Happiness + Find a Therapist, July 2007. <http://www.psychologytoday.com/blog/high-octane-women/201107/why-we-dread-and-so-often-fail-change>

Brown, Brené. "Want to Be Happy? Stop Trying to Be Perfect." *CNN*. Cable News Network, 12 Nov. 2010. <http://www.cnn.com/2010/LIVING/11/01/give.up.perfection/>

Bunnin, Nicholas, and Jiyuan Yu. *The Blackwell Dictionary of Western Philosophy*. Malden, MA: Blackwell Pub., 2004. Hendrickson, Robert. *The Encyclopedia of Word and Phrase Origins*. London: Macmillan, 1987.

Catton, William R. "The Problem of Denial." *www.zo.utexas.edu*. University of Texas, 1994. <http://www.zo.utexas.edu/courses/Thoc/Denial.source.html

Chan, Amanda L. "Why Learning Leads To Happiness." *The Huffington Post*. TheHuffingtonPost.com, 10 Apr. 2012. <http://www.huffingtonpost.com/2012/04/10/learning-happiness_n_1415568.html>

"China Demographics Profile 2014." *China Demographics Profile 2014*. CIA World Factbook, 23 Aug. 2014. http://www.indexmundi.com/china/demographics_profile.html

Cherry, Kendra. "Common Defense Mechanisms People Use to Cope with Anxiety." *Psychology.about.com*. About.com, n.d. <http://psychology.about.com/od/theoriesofpersonality/ss/

defensemech_3.htm>

Cohen, Matthew. "Top 20 Sports Records That Will Never Be Broken." *Wilt's 100 Points*. Bleacher Report, 22 Apr. 2012. <http://bleacherreport.com/articles/1151636-the-top-20-sports-records-that-will-never-be-broken>

"Conflict Diamonds." *Did Someone Die for That Diamond?* Amnesty International USA, 2013. <http://www.amnestyusa.org/our-work/issues/business-and-human-rights/oil-gas-and-mining-industries/conflict-diamonds>

Csikszentmihalyi, Mihaly. Finding Flow: The Psychology of Engagement with Everyday Life. New York: Basic, 1997.

Davidson, Donald. "Actions, Reasons, and Causes." *The Journal of Philosophy* 60.23, American Philosophical Association, Eastern Division, Sixtieth Annual Meeting (1963): 685-700.

"Description of the ACT." *Test Descriptions*. ACT, Inc., 2014. http://www.actstudent.org/testprep/descriptions/?_ga=1.130330511.10 26249024.1412000947

Dettmer, H. William., *The Logical Thinking Process: A Systems Approach to Complex Problem Solving*. Milwaukee, WI: ASQ Quality, 2007.

"Diamond 4Cs Education - Introduction." 4 Cs of Diamond Quality by GIA. Gemological Institute of America Inc., n.d. 2014. <http://gia4cs.gia.edu/EN-US/the-diamond-4-cs.htm?gclid=CIf7uLG4zc ACFcZQ7AodUFQAWw>.

Diesing, Paul. "Objectivism vs. Subjectivism in the Social Sciences."*Philosophy of Science* Vol. 33, No. 1/2 (Mar. - Jun., 1966), pp. 124-133. Published by: The University of Chicago Press

"Domino's 'Inspired New Pizza' Scores Big Win Against Papa John›s & Pizza Hut in National Taste Test." Press Release. Domino›s Investor Relations. Domino›s Pizza, 2 Feb. 2010. <http://phx.corporate-ir.net/phoenix.zhtml?c=135383&p=irol-newsArticle&ID=1381948&highlight=>

Editors. "The 100 Hottest Women of 2013." *@menshealthmag.*

Men'sHealth, 1 Feb. 2013. http://www.menshealth.com/sex-women/hottest-women-2013

Edwards, Tab. *Chocolate Peppers: Why Acting in Your Own Self-Interest is Good for You, Your Loved Ones, Society, and the World.* S.l.: TMBE, 2013.

Fitch, Frederick B. "The Perfection of Perfection." Ed. Sherwood J. B. Sugden.*Monist* 47.3 (1963): 466-71.

Gawlik, Marilyn E. "Variables Related to Perfectionism."*www.mckendree.edu.* McKendree University, <https://www.mckendree.edu/academics/scholars/issue18/gawlik.htm>

Gillham, D. G. "IDEAS OF HUMAN PERFECTION." *Theoria: A Journal of Social and Political Theory* No. 45 (1975): 13-27. *JSTOR.*

Goldratt, E. M. *Theory of Constraints.* The North River Press, 1990.

Greenspon, Thomas S. "Healthy Perfectionism" Is an Oxymoron! Reflections on the Psychology of Perfectionism and the Sociology of Science. *Journal of Secondary Gifted Education*, v11 n4 p197-208 Sum 2000

Greenwald, Rachel. *Why He Didn't Call You Back: 1,000 Guys Reveal What They Really Though about You after Your Date.* New York: Crown, 2009.

Hamachek, Don E. "Psychodynamics of normal and neurotic perfectionism." *Psychology: A Journal of Human Behavior*, Vol 15(1), Feb 1978, 27-33.

Hazony, Yoram. "An Imperfect God." *Opinionator An Imperfect God Comments.* N.p., 25 Nov. 2012. <http://opinionator.blogs.nytimes.com/2012/11/25/an-imperfect-god/?_php=true&_type=blogs&_r=0>

"Hearts On Fire Dream Offset Signature Solitaire Engagement Ring." *Hearts On Fire.* N.p., n.d. 06 Jul. 2014. <http://www.heartsonfire.com/shop-jewelry/rings/engagement-rings/dream-offset-signature-solitaire-engagement-ring.aspx>

Hewitt, Paul L., Gordon L. Flett, and Cathy Weber. "Dimensions of Perfectionism and Suicide Ideation." *Cognitive Therapy and*

*Research*18.5 (1994): 439-60.

Holy Bible: English Standard Version. Wheaton, IL: Crossway Bibles, 2001.

Holy Bible, New International Version, Copyright © 1973, 1978, 1984, 2011 by Biblica, Inc.

"India's Population 2014." - *Population of India 2014- Current Population of India in 2014*. India Pages Online, n.d. http://www.indiaonlinepages.com/population/india-current-population.html

"Jade Mountain Resort Hotel, St. Lucia/Soufriere." *Jade Mountain Resort (St. Lucia/Soufriere)*. Trip Advisor, 29 Aug. 2012. 02 Nov. 2014. <http://www.tripadvisor.com/Hotel_Review-g147345-d623374-Reviews-Jade_Mountain_Resort-Soufriere_Soufriere_Quarter_St_Lucia.html#REVIEWS>

Kragen, Pam. "5 Local Teens Earn Perfect ACT Scores." *The San Diego Union-Tribune*. N.p., 8 June 2014. <http://www.utsandiego.com/news/2014/jun/08/5l-teens-earn-perfect-act-scores/>

Krueger, Joachim I. "Seligman's Flourish: The Second Coming Flourish: A Visionary New Understanding of Happiness and Well-Being Seligman Martin E. P. Free Press New York, NY." *The American Journal of Psychology* 125.1 (2012): 121-24.

Kuban, Adam. "Domino›s Changes Core Pizza Recipe." *Slice. seriouseats.com*. Slice, 16 Dec. 2009. <http://slice.seriouseats.com/archives/2009/12/dominos-pizza-changes-core-recipe-garlic-parsley-crust-sweeter-sauce-provolone-cheese.html>

Laozi, and Yutang Lin. *Laozi Dao De Jing = The Sayings of Lao-tzu ; a New Translation of the Tao Te Ching*. Taibei Xian Xindian Shi: Wen Zhi Chu Ban She, 1983.

LeVan, AJ. "Seeing Is Believing: The Power of Visualization." *Psychology Today*. N.p., 3 Dec. 2009. <http://www.psychologytoday.com/blog/flourish/200912/seeing-is-believing-the-power-visualization>

Lorde, Audre. *Sister Outsider: Essays and Speeches*. Freedom, CA.: Crossing Press. 1984.

Lyubomirsky, Sonja, Laura King, and Ed Diener. "The Benefits of Frequent Positive Affect: Does Happiness Lead to Success?" *Psychological Bulletin* 131.6 (2005): 803-55.

"Major Religions of the World Ranked by Number of Adherents." *Major Religions Ranked by Size*. N.p., 2005. <http://www.adherents.com/Religions_By_Adherents.html>

MailOnline, Bianca London for. "The Perfect Man DOES Exist ... in Fact There Are FIVE of Them out There!" *Mail Online*. Associated Newspapers, 14 Dec. 2012. <http://www.dailymail.co.uk/femail/article-2247988/The-perfect-man-DOES-exist--fact-FIVE-types-there.html>

Margolis, Joseph. "Objectivism and Relativism." *Proceedings of the Aristotelian Society*. New Series, Vol. 85, (1984 - 1985), pp. 171-19. Published by: The Aristotelian Society

Maslow, A. H. "A Theory of Human Motivation." Psychological Review, 50, 370-396. 1943.

Maslow, Abraham H. *Motivation and Personality*. New York: Harper. 1954.

McCloskey, H. J. "Objectivism in Aesthetics." *Ethics*. Vol. 74, No. 1 (Oct., 1963), pp. 61-64. Published by: The University of Chicago Press

McLeod, Saul. "Maslow's Hierarchy of Needs." Simply Psychology. 2007. www.simplypsychology.org/maslow.html

"Movies Made." *IMDb.com*., 2014. http://www.imdb.com/stats

"Overcome The 5 Main Reasons People Resist Change." *Forbes*. Forbes Magazine, 26 Nov. 2012. 02 Nov. 2014. <http://www.forbes.com/sites/lisaquast/2012/11/26/overcome-the-5-main-reasons-people-resist-change/>

Pacht, A. R. (1984). "Reflections on perfection." *American Psychologist*, 39, 386–390. Parker, W. (1997). "An empirical typology of perfectionism in academically talented children." *American Educational Research Journal*, 34, 545–562.

Parker, Robert. "About the Wine Advocate." ERobertParker.com.

<http://www.erobertparker.com/info/WineAdvocate.asp>

Parker, Robert. "Robert Parker's Rating System." E. RobertParker. com. 2014. <http://www.erobertparker.com/info/legend.asp>

Parker, Robert. "Robert Parker, The Wine Advocate." *The Wine Advocate.* <http://www.wine-searcher.com/critics-27-robert+park er+the+wine+advocate>

"The Perfect Woman." *The 60 Minutes/Vanity Fair Poll: The Perfect Woman.* Vanity Fair, Sept. 2013. <http://www.vanityfair.com/ magazine/2013/09/ten-percent-female-boss-poll_slideshow_ item8_9>

"Perfectionism." *Psychology Today: Health, Help, Happiness + Find a Therapist.* Psychology Today, n.d. 02 Sept. 2014

"Perfectionism versus Healthy Striving." *Cmhc.utexas.edu.* University of Texas at Austin Counseling and Mental Health Center, <http:// cmhc.utexas.edu/perfectionism.html>

Percy, Pam. *The Field Guide to Chickens.* St. Paul, MN: Voyageur, 2006.

"Phobias: MedlinePlus." *Fear of Public Speaking.* U.S. National Library of Medicine, n.d. <http://www.nlm.nih.gov/medlineplus/ phobias.html>

"Rare Disease Makes Girl Unable to Feel Pain."*nbcnews.com.* NBC News, 1 Sept. 2004. <http://www.nbcnews.com/id/6379795/ ns/health-childrens_health/t/rare-disease-makes-girl-unable-feel-pain/#.VC_z2PldWVM>

"Relativism." Definition of in Oxford Dictionary (British & World English). 2014. <http://www.oxforddictionaries.com/definition/ english/relativism>

Rettner, Rachael. "The Dark Side of Perfectionism Revealed." *LiveScience.* TechMedia Network, 11 July 2010. <http://www.livescience.com/6724-dark-side-perfectionism-revealed.html>

Rossignol, Pascal. "Sixty Percent of Adults Can't Digest Milk - USATODAY.com. *USA Today*, 15 Sept. 2009. http://usatoday30.

usatoday.com/tech/science/2009-08-30-lactose-intolerance_N. htm

Rudrauf, Lucien. "Perfection." *The Journal of Aesthetics and Art Criticism*23.1, In Honor of Thomas Munro (1964): 123-30.

Schwartz, Mel. *The Art of Intimacy, the Pleasure of Passion: A Journey into Soulful Relationships.* Chappaqua, NY: Quantum, 1999.

Schwatrz, Mel. "The Problem with Perfection." *Psychology Today.* 30 Nov. 2008. <http://www.psychologytoday.com/blog/shift-mind/200811/the-problem-perfection>

"Seeking Perfection." *BBC News: Science: Human Body & Mind.* BBC, <http://www.bbc.co.uk/science/humanbody/mind/articles/ personalityandindividuality/perfectionism.shtml>

Seltzer, Leon F. "The Path to Unconditional Self-Acceptance." *Psychology Today: Health, Help, Happiness + Find a Therapist.* 9 Sept. 2008. <http://www.psychologytoday.com/ blog/evolution-the-self/200809/the-path-unconditional-self-acceptance>

"Sexiest Men: The Results." *Sexiest Men – 100 Hottest Men in the World Results (Glamour.com UK).* Glamour, 7 Jan. 2014. <http://www. glamourmagazine.co.uk/celebrity/celebrity-galleries/2013/07/ sexiest-hottest-men-of-2013>

St. Louis, Kenneth O. "A Global Project to Measure Public Attitudes About Stuttering." *The ASHA Leader.* American Speech-Language-Hearing Association. October 18, 2005

Staff, Mayo Clinic. "Denial: When It Helps, When It Hurts."*www. mayoclinic.org.* Mayo Clinic, n.d. <http://www.mayoclinic.org/ healthy-living/adult-health/in-depth/denial/art-20047926>

"Underdogs: The Bloodhound's Amazing Sense of Smell." *www.pbs. org, Nature.* PBS, n.d. <http://www.pbs.org/wnet/nature/episodes/ underdogs/the-bloodhounds-amazing-sense-of-smell/350/>

Wade, Brandon. "The 5 Things Successful Men Notice First in a Woman." *The Huffington Post.* TheHuffingtonPost.com, 31 Oct. 2012. <http://www.huffingtonpost.com/brandon-wade/dating-

advice_b_2049249.html>

Warren, Rick. "We Are Not Perfect, But Our God Is." *We Are Not Perfect, But Our God Is*. N.p., 21 May 2014. <http://rickwarren. org/devotional/english/we-are-not-perfect-but-our-god-is>

Weiss, Jeffrey. "Do Christians, Muslims and Jews Worship the Same God?" *CNN Belief Blog RSS*. N.p., 1 Sept. 2013. <http://religion. blogs.cnn.com/2013/09/01/do-christians-muslims-and-jews-worship-the-same-god/>

"Which Animal Has the Most Tastebuds?" *Info.com*. N.p., n.d. <http:// topics.info.com/Which-animal-has-the-most-tastebuds_1445>

"Wilt's 100-Point Game Box Score." *Sixers*. National Basketball Association, 2 Mar. 1962. <http://www.nba.com/sixers/news/ wilt_boxscore.html>

Wolchover, Natalie. "What If Humans Had Eagle Vision?" *LiveScience*. TechMedia Network, 24 Feb. 2012. <http://www.livescience. com/18658-humans-eagle-vision.html>

Index